FROM BLIND MAN
TO IRONMAN

Dear Paul,

Keep running!

FROM BLIND MAN TO IRONMAN

HASEEB AHMAD

Matador
9 Priory Business Park,
Wistow Road, Kibworth Beauchamp,
Leicestershire. LE8 0RX
Tel: 0116 279 2299
Email: books@troubador.co.uk
Web: www.troubador.co.uk/matador
Twitter: @matadorbooks

ISBN 978 1788033 305

British Library Cataloguing in Publication Data.
A catalogue record for this book is available from the British Library.

Printed and bound by CPI Group (UK) Ltd, Croydon, CR0 4YY
Typeset in 11pt Minion Pro by Troubador Publishing Ltd, Leicester, UK

Matador is an imprint of Troubador Publishing Ltd

MIX
Paper from
responsible sources
FSC
www.fsc.org
FSC® C013604

Dedication

First and foremost I would like to dedicate this book to my wonderful daughter, Ayeisha, who has brought me so much happiness over the years she has been on this earth. I dedicate this for her to believe that anything is possible, whatever the challenges ahead, given the right amount of patience and determination. I'd also like to thank my incredible wife, Mary, for all of her marvellous and unfailing support and kindness to me over the 27 years we have been together, without which I wouldn't be the man I am today.

I also want to thank from the bottom of my heart all of my guides who, over the past few years, have helped me achieve some unbelievable goals and the collection of medals which lines the bottom of my wardrobe! I hope our friendships will endure and, whether they do or not, rest assured that you guys will never be forgotten. You are now immortalised in this book!

Last, but not least, thanks to all those wonderful people who have given me feedback on this personal journey. I could so easily have spent much longer on this dedication and acknowledged many more special individuals in my life, but one has to stop somewhere in order to get the book published.

Haseeb Ahmed
June 2017

CONTENTS

FOREWORD

In writing the foreword to this book I deliberated over what makes Haseeb Ahmad such a special individual, and what makes others line up to guide him – and, on occasion, drag him – to the finish line.

I knew it went far beyond any athletic talents he may have, and eventually I was reminded of two interviews I conducted recently in my work as a journalist. On both occasions I closed the discussion by asking the subjects what advice they would give to anyone struggling in life. They both responded with identical answers: "Ask for help."

Three short words, but ones that too many of us misinterpret as a sign of weakness, often born out of the mistaken belief that it is wrong to burden others with your troubles. If life teaches us anything, it is that none of us has all the answers; yet reaching out shows not only humility, but strength. A simple premise, but one it took me years to grasp. Not so Haseeb.

Of course, it would be easy to say he doesn't have a choice. Having lost his sight as a teenager, Haseeb is reliant on his family for assistance with day-to-day matters, and guides for his athletic pursuits. But while true on a practical level, Haseeb can choose his attitude, and decreed early in life that failing vision would not be an excuse for self-pity, but a challenge to be conquered every day – and that through his studies, his work, his family, and his sport, there would be the sparkle of adventure along the way.

What's more, when others offer an arm to help, it is far from a sacrifice, but the chance to channel our own energies into a cause from which we too benefit. I've taken part in many races, but none have been so rewarding as those I've run in a fluorescent yellow singlet with GUIDE screen-printed on the back, and Haseeb alongside me for every step.

I first gave him my arm in early 2015, shortly after I'd responded to a speculative tweet by Braddan Johnson, who had set up the website guiderunning.uk to help pair visually impaired athletes with suitable guides. I'd driven from Gloucestershire on a frosty morning to find Has' street in Oadby on a west-facing slope and the pavements with a glassy sheen.

Grass would offer a softer landing for the predictable teething problems, so we headed to a local playing field and he produced an impressively sturdy leather tether tailor-made for the job. I would never see it again. I think, given his untimely ability to misplace this one vital piece of kit, we ran most of the races gripping either end of a shoelace.

No matter, we started gently, using his tried and tested Chuckle Brothers technique – "To me, to you" – and within ten minutes I realised his credentials as an athlete far outstripped my own. I also recall thinking just how perceptive he was of his surroundings when I negotiated an open gate and he gently suggested we needed to move a little further my way next time.

"How did you know?" I asked.

"The gatepost just whacked my hand."

A fortnight later I returned to jog alongside the A6 in Leicestershire – the breeding ground of champions – on another chilly Sunday morning. When running with Haseeb you lend not only your eyes, but your ear, and, as the juggernauts thundered past, didn't he ever chew it off. If there is one thing I learned quickly about my dear friend, it's his unrivalled ability to natter.

Fast-forward fourteen months and the two of us were again united by a tether, only this time in a field of forty thousand for the Virgin Money London Marathon. I'll leave Haseeb to dissect that one in the pages that follow, but my most vivid memories are not of the race itself, but the journey we took to get there.

The Cambridge Half-Marathon in February was our first race together, and also a debut for his daughter, Ayeisha. It was the furthest she had run and the nerves were palpable, yet the highlight was seeing her reunited with her proud father and mother Mary having completed the distance far faster than she thought possible.

In Reading, a final race before London, we planned to adhere to a strict pace for the first ten miles before a fast descent around the five-mile mark saw Haseeb throw caution to the wind and let those little legs whirl. We hurtled down that hill at sub-five-minute-mile pace, the speed increasing with every step. The sensible decision would have been to rein it in and save ourselves for the later miles, but emboldened by the rush of the wind and the surge of endorphins, it was a gloriously carefree moment; a metaphor for how Haseeb approaches life – facing the fear of the dark, and still surging forth.

It can be contagious. The simultaneous gasp and then roar of the crowd as we entered the Madejski Stadium and almost took a tumble on the sharp incline shows how his endeavours inspire others. He is not just blazing a trail for blind runners and triathletes, but helping to change wider perceptions about disabilities.

Finally, at the start of 2016, with my own mental health faltering, I needed a reason to get out of bed. Along with my two daughters, Rachel and Laura, Haseeb provided that. There is so much that is arbitrary in running 26.2 miles, and trying to achieve that prescribed distance, yet it provided me with a sense of duty and responsibility when I was struggling to order my thoughts. He thanked me countless times for guiding him in those races, but the bigger debt will always be mine.

If anyone reading this is thinking of giving guiding a go, I urge you to pick up the tether and take those first steps. It will be the start of a unique relationship and while you may be attached for just a few hours, you will form an unbreakable bond for life.

Tim Heming
Sports Journalist

PROLOGUE

Eleven hours after I started the Ironman race in Barcelona I was three minutes from finishing. I could hear the crowds shouting and cheering the athletes who had finished ahead of me and the closer we got, the louder the cheering got.

Dunc, my guide, was also shouting and whooping as we ran down the carpeted Finishing Chute, "You've done it, mate, you're a world record holder!"

Paul Kaye's voice bellowed from the PA system as he bigged up each and every athlete who crossed the finishing line.

I couldn't wait to cross that line. Every step was a step closer to not suffering any more. My whole body was racked with pain, and every cell in my body was screaming out for me to just stop.

As I crossed the finishing line, Paul Kaye shouted out, "Haseeb Ahmad, you are an Ironman and a world record-breaker!"

I stopped running immediately after I stepped over the finishing line and my legs gave way. I was utterly exhausted and spent. I felt arms around me to hold me up. I felt so weak, I could hardly talk. I was assisted to the medical tent where I spent the next twenty minutes or so lying on a canvas stretcher with a bin next to me in case I threw up. I felt extremely ill but had nothing in my stomach to throw up.

I got no sympathy from Dunc, a hardened multi-Ironman finisher who had been to the World Championships in 2015, completing it in a highly impressive time of just over ten hours. The fact that I am blind made no difference to him. His job was done, I was alive and he wanted to get me out of the medical tent and reunited with my family who were there to support me.

Still feeling extremely ill he guided me out of the tent and we walked through the athletes' lounge. We got a standing ovation from our fellow athletes. It was both wonderful and humbling. I, with the superb guiding of Dunc, had smashed the world record by almost seven minutes. Yet, I couldn't enjoy that moment. I had put everything into the race and it was payback time. Waves of nausea swept over me as officials, friends and family came over to congratulate me. I just wanted the sick feeling to go away, and to have a lie down somewhere nice and quiet.

What followed in the days and months after the world record took me completely by surprise. But what is even more remarkable, having lost my sight in my youth, when the whole world seemed to collapse around me, is that here I was, on top of the world!

CHAPTER 1

THE MAKINGS OF A BLIND IRONMAN

Having broken the world record for the fastest Ironman completed by a blind man on 2nd October 2016, at the age of forty-six, I wanted to share my journey of adventure, overcoming adversity, and why I decided to do it in the first place. My amazing story will inspire you to believe that anything is possible.

The Ironman consists of a 2.4-mile swim, a 112-mile bike ride (on a tandem for me) and a 26.2-mile run (marathon). And yes, it is one discipline straight after the other. And yes, I do it with the help of a guide, who has to be fitter than me. I am tethered on the swim, do the bike leg on a tandem and tethered on the run.

However, I wasn't always blind. My sight deteriorated over a number of years from the age of ten. Neither was I a triathlete as a youngster. In fact the first time I ever heard of a triathlon was watching one on TV in 1988 before I lost my sight completely, thinking, *What a crazy sport. Why on earth would you want to do a long swim, then an extremely long bike ride and then a marathon at the end of that? Clearly these people need their heads examining!* No, it wasn't for me. I didn't really give it much thought after that for almost thirty years.

My story begins forty-six years before breaking the record time set in the *Guinness Book of World Records*. I was born on the 3rd November 1969 in Wolverhampton. My parents, of

Pakistani birth, had come to the UK in 1968, like many other people from the Commonwealth, for a better life and the opportunities England had to offer. My father came to train as a teacher, and went on to study at the teacher training college in Wolverhampton. My parents were lodging with friends of theirs in a small room when I came along. I was told that when I was born my mum took one look at me and started crying as I was a little wrinkly and less than beautiful! She soon fell in love with me though – how could she not? Thankfully, I did turn into a very cute baby as I recall from seeing pictures of myself before I lost my sight altogether. My dad was a keen photographer and took a great deal of pictures of me and the rest of our family. As a sighted child I loved leafing through the photograph albums. I remember particularly how beautiful my mum looked in her very colourful traditional Pakistani outfits.

About a year after I was born, my father managed to get a teaching job in London. He bought a house in Brixton which required a lot of work. When I was less than a year old my father decided to send me to Pakistan to stay with my Uncle Latif, who was married to my dad's sister Auntie Kaneez. My mum didn't really have much of a say in the matter (she told me years later), and naturally she was very upset at the time. I'm sure my father's intentions were good and, to be honest, I don't know the exact details of why this was done other than to make it easier for my parents to get on with the major work needed on their new home. A couple of months after being sent to Pakistan though, I became very ill, and my Auntie Kaneez and Uncle Latif brought me back to London to be reunited with my parents.

Soon after my return, the 9th January 1971 saw the arrival of my brother Toseef. There is a great photo of me around two years old, crying because I had finished my ice cream while my brother was still eating his. Apparently I wanted more ice cream. Early evidence of a sweet tooth which remains to this day.

I was two and a half years old when my brother and I were taken to Pakistan again. This time my understanding is that my mum wasn't coping very well with us. I was told, years later, that she had once left Toseef in the park in his pushchair. I know now that in actual fact she was suffering from postnatal depression. I know that there wasn't a great deal of help or sympathy for mental health issues back then, and maybe my parents weren't able to access any help that was available. In any case, off we went, my brother and I, to Pakistan to be looked after by my grandparents, uncles and aunts. Once again, my mum didn't have much say in the matter. She remained in England with my father while I travelled in the arms of my dad's sister and her husband. When my mum talks about this now she gets very tearful and upset. She didn't have any control over the situation. My father made all the decisions about family affairs and this was no exception.

I have very vague but happy memories of Pakistan. My grandparents were lovely. My grandfather ran a small shop in a village called Kasoor in the Punjabi region, about thirty miles from Lahore, just inside the border with India. The village was small, although, to me as an infant, the streets and houses seemed huge. The streets were cobbled and there were open gutters where the sewage from the houses flowed freely. It was extremely hot, dusty and there were always plenty of flies buzzing around. Thinking back, it was very underdeveloped by Western living standards. Many people were living a hand-to-mouth existence. However, my father's family were pretty well off compared to other village folk and indeed they were extremely charitable to family and friends.

My grandparents' house seemed large to me. It had three storeys set around three sides of an open courtyard. There was no sewerage system in Pakistan, so the toilet was on the top floor, which was an open, flat rooftop. There were people who would come regularly to muck out the toilets. I remember, even as an infant, I found it quite stomach-churning.

While my grandfather was very busy running his little shop and ensuring that the family was being supported financially, my grandmother took care of the house. She was a real contrast to my grandfather. Whilst my grandfather was very loving towards my brother and me, he was known for his stern but fair approach. My grandmother was really kind and gentle. I very rarely heard her raise her voice.

I know that my mum did come and visit us on a few occasions when my parents could afford the flight to Pakistan. As I was constantly provided with all the love and attention I needed by my grandparents, aunts and uncles I didn't really know any different and can't remember missing my mum or dad.

The four years I was in Pakistan are full of fond memories. I remember, when it got really hot (and it did get really hot in the summer months), sleeping on the wicker rather than the mattress of the wooden-framed beds. Not very comfortable. There was no air conditioning of course, so sleeping in the open air under the shade was the only way of keeping cool in the extreme heat. Everyone slept during the hottest part of the day for a couple of hours at least. My aunts and uncles used to encourage us to sleep, but being little kids with lots of energy, my brother and I didn't quite see the point. If you weren't tired, why go to bed? So, we would just pretend until the adults went to sleep, then get up and start playing.

I must have been around three years old when, on one occasion, I decided to leave the house by myself. My grandmother was frantic with worry. All the family were looking for me everywhere and couldn't find me in the house. Then someone had the presence of mind to check whether I was at my grandfather's shop. There I was, sitting with him having a bottle of Coke! I had slipped out of the house and, remembering where my grandfather kept his shop, made my own way there.

There were also a couple of accidents that I had while in Pakistan. One such incident occurred when my Auntie Nasreen's fiancé decided to take me out on his motorcycle. I was around four years old at the time and very excited about the prospect of getting to ride on the motorcycle. Of course I didn't have a helmet or any form of protective clothing. During the journey I vaguely remember looking down and seeing blood coming from my foot. Somehow the wheel of the motorcycle had started to rub against my ankle, cutting through my skin. My future uncle-in-law looked down, spotted the blood and rushed me to hospital where I was stitched up and bandaged. Apparently when my foot was being ground down by the wheel of the bike I didn't cry or make a fuss. I obviously have a high pain threshold! I think that I was very lucky not to get a far worse injury – I often think I am fortunate to only have a scar to show for the incident.

I had another accident while in Pakistan which was far more serious and cause for concern for my grandparents and family. This happened when I was happily playing with my cousins who lived next door. I tripped, fell down some stairs and knocked my head against the stone floor. I was unconscious for a few days. According to the doctors I was seriously concussed and only time would tell whether I would pull through. Needless to say I did, and I don't think there was any long-term damage! Yet, when I reflect back, I do wonder whether the fall was a consequence of my very poor eyesight which wasn't picked up until I came back to England at the age of five.

In 1975, my father came to take my brother and me back to the UK. My first recollection of not being able to see very well was upon reaching the arrivals lounge after the flight home. I caught sight of someone who I thought was my mum. I wasn't standing too far away from her and my father was very surprised that I didn't recognise her as my Auntie Kaneez.

"No, that's your auntie, not your mum. She is waiting for you at home."

He told us that when we got home there would be lots of surprises for us, and he wasn't kidding. We were taken upstairs to my parents' bedroom, a large, bay-windowed room on the first floor of the house. To my utter delight, strewn across the floor were toys galore including Lego, toy cars and puzzles. This was long before the days of computer games and consoles. I felt overwhelming love for my parents for buying so many presents. I was so, so happy.

CHAPTER 2

TIME FOR SCHOOL

It didn't feel as though I had much time at home after coming back from Pakistan before it was time for my first day at school. I was five years old at the time. My parents walked me down to Holy Trinity Primary School, which was only fifteen minutes from our house. It was all a bit of a shock to the system really. I don't remember being prepared at all for the overwhelming experience of going to my first school. Toseef, my younger brother by a year and two months, went to preschool where he started on half-days to begin with, whereas I was dropped off and started school full-time.

My first day was a bit strange. At the same time as I was being escorted to my classroom by my parents there was another child, a little girl, also being dropped off. As soon as her parents left her, she ran from the classroom crying and calling for her mummy. Her parents turned around and took her back home. I thought I would try the same tactic. When I started to cry, though, running back in the direction from which we had come, my parents were nowhere to be seen. Rather embarrassed, I had to return to the classroom.

My first teacher was lovely. She introduced me to another boy, an Afro-Caribbean lad called Leon Francis, who took me under his wing. He showed me around the classroom and took care of me in the playground. He told me that if ever I was in trouble, to just shout out his name and he would come running. I tested this out a couple of times when I was being bullied and he kept to his word. Leon was my guardian angel.

As I had only just arrived back from Pakistan, my English was non-existent, and there were some misunderstandings while I was trying to get to grips with the language and culture. One day, I was trying to communicate the number two to a girl in the class. I stuck two fingers up at her with my palm facing towards me. She went straight to the teacher to say that I swore at her. Five minutes of standing in the corner was my punishment. I had no idea what was going on!

I can't remember being especially unhappy at school; nor can I remember looking forward to going. One morning my mum gave my brother and me a glass of extra-hot milk. We had these weird red plastic tumblers that she used to serve us our milk in. Maybe it was the red that made the milk extra hot this particular morning, but I was having trouble drinking it quickly, and I knew we would be late for school – we'd be sent to the head teacher for sure. I kept complaining to my mum but she insisted we finish our milk. We drank up, Toseef and I, and got ready for school, and when we got there we were both sent to the head for our tardiness.

When the head teacher asked us why we were late I just told him the truth: "My mum made us drink our milk but it was too hot and took ages to finish." I expected the head teacher to be really cross with us; instead he fell about laughing. I, on the other hand, was confused.

I got my first taste of racism when I went to primary school. I was often called 'Paki', or told to go back to my own country. As I was only five years old when I first heard this I just didn't understand it at first. Looking back, I guess both Toseef and I were different. We had just arrived from Pakistan and must have seemed a bit out of the ordinary. The taunts and racist abuse didn't come from my classmates, however, but older children.

But I loved playing with other kids and joined in the various games that we played at break time. Once, while playing tag I tripped and somehow managed to catch the chin of a lad who had just had stitches put into his lower jaw due to an accident he had had at home. I was horrified as the stitches came open due to my fingers catching the edge of the wound. He was really understanding about it, probably because he was sent home early. I was to meet him years later at secondary school, when he fondly recalled the incident.

I also witnessed a shocking incident which, even at the age of five, I knew was just wrong. It was time for PE and we were all changing in the classroom, both boys and girls. All of a sudden I heard the teacher shouting at a little black girl that her leotard was inside out. This was a different teacher to the one who had welcomed me to the school when I first started. This teacher made the little girl stand on top of the table and take it off; then put it on the right way round. I averted my eyes. I felt ashamed and just couldn't believe what was happening. The poor girl was extremely distressed and in floods of tears. I'm not sure what happened to the teacher but can't actually remember her being around for the rest of that year. I really hope that the little girl got over the trauma of what happened.

I was at Holy Trinity for about five years. In that time my eyesight was poor, but to all intents and purposes, I seemed to be coping okay. My father had taken us to the optician to have our eyes tested and I was given glasses. There must have been some concern as both Toseef and I were referred to the staff at St Thomas' Eye Hospital who regularly checked our eyes, changed the prescription of my lenses and then gave both of us a clean bill of health. According to my dad, the doctors even said that we would be able to drive a car with the level of eyesight we had. Even at the age of five I recall feeling a sense of relief and reassurance at this good news. I remember being able to read the first four lines of the chart.

Without my glasses I could hardly see as I was naturally very short-sighted, but with them, I could pretty much manage to do everything that any other boy or girl of my age was doing: riding bikes, playing ball games, drawing, reading and writing. It wasn't until I was around ten years old that I noticed I was having a few problems seeing the blackboard, even from the front of the class. I hadn't noticed this before. Maybe it was just that we hadn't done a lot of blackboard work until this point. I told my dad and he advised me to sit closer to the front or tell the teacher. I did both, but I can't remember being offered any additional help. Maybe the teacher thought I was making it up.

I really enjoyed PE and managed the best I could as the teacher always insisted I took off my bog-standard NHS glasses. I remember one particular PE lesson when I was playing rounders. It was my turn to bat and I really couldn't see the ball coming at me at all. I swung the bat anyway... *thwack!* By some incredible miracle my bat had connected with the ball and it went flying. The teacher was elated. It was a girl who batted next and she swung the bat and missed.

To my delight the teacher said, "Come on, you can do better than that. Even Haseeb can hit the ball and he didn't even have his glasses on."

Away from school, Toseef and I spent a lot of time playing with my cousins Yasmin, Jawad and Shazad. My Auntie Kaneez, Uncle Latif and their three children were the only other family we had in the UK so we spent a lot of time together. We were really close. They lived in Streatham, which is only a short car ride away, and as teenagers we used to bike across in no time.

I also recall playing a lot of board games including Monopoly, Scrabble and Cluedo, and one of my favourites was chess, which my dad had taught me to play. I loved challenging my brother to a game of chess as I used to beat him on a regular basis. My dad wasn't so easy to beat. In fact I can't ever remember winning against him. I was extremely competitive at a very young age. Winning was important to me.

When we were primary school age I have great memories of playing imaginary games with my cousins at all the birthday parties and sleepovers we had. My Auntie Kaneez was great and loved having us around. In the morning, if we were staying over, she would always do us a cooked breakfast which involved sweet eggy bread. I'm not sure this is a traditional Pakistani breakfast. In fact I'm convinced it's not. And as disgusting as it might sound, we absolutely loved it.

Every Saturday and Sunday we had to go to Streatham mosque. It wasn't so bad to start off with, but it got really boring as we entered our teenage years. The teaching methods in those days involved shouting at the kids or hitting them with a stick if they read their Quranic verses incorrectly. The *Molvi* (priest) seemed to target the youngest children. He would smack their hands with a stick if they weren't concentrating and they would burst out crying. So wrong, and they certainly (quite rightly) wouldn't get away with it today.

Most of the staff who worked at the mosque seemed authoritarian and out of touch. Later, when I was around fourteen years old, our parents would drop us off at the mosque gates. We'd wait until they went home and then sneak down to the shops and wander around for a couple of hours until it was time to be picked up. We were eventually found out, much to the dismay of our parents.

Throughout my childhood, my dad – being a teacher and, of course, of Pakistani background (a fatal combination) – would insist on spending copious time with my brother and me, drilling us in our times tables and spelling. He would get so cross if I got my times tables wrong or my homework wasn't to a high standard. I hated him in those moments, but I also remember him being very loving and it wasn't unknown for him to often cuddle and kiss both myself and my brother. I remember having overwhelming feelings of love and affection for both my parents.

When I was ten years old my father told us that he had got a job teaching in Zambia and that we would be leaving to go to Africa in the summer of 1980. I was really excited. It felt like we were about to embark on the adventure of a lifetime! It was an incredible experience. One I will never forget.

CHAPTER 3

ZAMBIA

The prospect of living in Zambia was really exciting for both Toseef and me. I wasn't sure what to expect, but even then I had this great sense of adventure. I loved the fact that I was leaving school to travel to a completely different country while all my friends would have to go back in the following year. They gave me a great send-off; wishing me good luck and giving me presents.

When we arrived into Zambia it was extremely humid and there were long queues for passport control; comforting that some things don't change much over time. Of course in those days security wasn't so tight.

We headed for the hotel. I was ten years old and everything was just amazing, including the prospect of staying in Zambia's only five-star offering: the Intercontinental Taj Pamodzi in Lusaka, the capital city. We stayed at the hotel for what seemed like months, but was probably only several weeks, while my father was waiting to find out where he would be posted for his teaching job. In the meantime, we spent many days soaking up the sights and sounds of Lusaka. We made friends with another family who had two kids the same age as us. There was a little girl around my age who we played with and my dad insisted on teasing me that she was my girlfriend. I really hated that!

My dad was eventually posted to Isoka, 563 miles from

Lusaka in the north of Zambia. It was a long and tortuous journey involving trains, planes and automobiles. We stayed in numerous hotels on what seemed like an epic journey which took over a week. The hotels we stayed in weren't too bad, but obviously not as good as the Pamodzi!

In one hotel we stayed at, there was a large recreational room where my brother and I took our remote-control cars. They didn't last long as the dust and dirt surrounding the hotel soon got into the motors and they stopped working. As basic as the cars were, they were great fun. However, for some reason that I couldn't work out at the age of ten, the cars only turned left. And, eventually, they didn't turn at all!

Despite my poor eyesight I can still recall seeing the tiny lizards which ran up the outside of the hotel walls, the giant beetles which were the size of my dad's palms and the copious amount of flies. We had to take our daily malaria tablets. We also heard horror stories of a fly, the human botfly, which could bury its eggs in your skin where the larvae then grew, feeding off their host, until they matured and broke out of the person's skin. Not the kind of story you want to hear at any age.

My brother and I coped quite well with the journey considering our age, but it must have been extremely stressful for both my parents, especially my mum. As Muslims we couldn't eat meat that wasn't sacrificed in the name of Allah, and getting halal meat in Zambia was nigh on impossible. There were a few occasions when my parents found it difficult to get hold of food and/or accommodation, but somehow things seemed to work out.

When we eventually got to Isoka, we stayed for a short time with another family – a couple and their son, who must have been around eight years old. I don't think they particularly liked us staying there, and I don't quite know what the arrangement was, but my parents eventually secured a house on the complex assigned to the teaching staff. I believe it was one of the better houses as it remained in quite good condition, though we had no fridge. If we had any meat it had to be stored in the refrigerator in the house belonging to the head teacher. My brother and I were once sent down to collect the meat from the head teacher's house. As we approached the house, we could see a rather vicious-looking dog in the garden. I was petrified. I wasn't used to dogs and had been chased by strays a few times in London. One of the head teacher's kids appeared and wasn't particularly friendly. Eventually, I managed to persuade her that the meat in the fridge belonged to us and she reluctantly handed it over. When I got back home I told my mum that I was never going back there again! I think she thought I was being rather silly.

My dad decided to keep chickens. They seemed to live a very happy existence around the house. Happy, that is, until one day he told me that we were going to slaughter one for dinner and I was going to help him. I was horrified. He managed to catch one and asked me to hold its legs while he chopped its head off. As Muslims, there is a religious way in which animals are slaughtered; by cutting the jugular vein whilst repeating, three times over in Arabic, that God is great. Well, I held the chicken's legs while my dad started to cut its throat. I just wasn't strong enough to hold on to the legs and let go. I found out what it means when people talk about 'running around like a headless chicken'. My dad was none too happy. I think he eventually tracked it down and we had a rather nice chicken curry that evening.

It was also around this time when my brother had his accident. He was playing with one of our friends, running around the house. I was inside at the time when I heard the commotion outside. Toseef had fallen and broken his arm.

When my dad got back from work the first thing he did was to start shouting at me, "What have you done to your brother?!"

Typical – I always got the blame when my brother got hurt. I was really upset at the false allegation. I tried to explain that it had nothing to do with me and I was nowhere near him when he hurt himself. When eventually he realised that it was just an accident, Toseef was taken to the local hospital where the doctor did his best to put his arm in a cast. Unfortunately there was no X-ray machine available, and my dad had to take Toseef to the nearest hospital with all the specialist equipment, which was a couple of hundred miles away. It was something that my dad could have done without. My brother was very lucky not to have lost his arm, as the break was very serious.

During our time in Zambia my father was very keen that we didn't miss out on our education. Even through the summer holidays he would get us to sit down and study, which often involved going through maths books, doing sums or remembering our times tables. He managed to find a really good maths teacher, who was from Holland, to teach my brother and me some maths. I remember having a few lessons which I did actually enjoy. He also managed to find a guitar teacher, so I had a couple of lessons in that too. Unfortunately, I could never really get to grips with the guitar. At ten years old, my hands were simply too small and weak to hold the strings down.

One of the most amazing things I recall is when my father had arranged for us to stay with a friend of his who lived near Livingstone to visit Victoria Falls. The way in which the falls were formed is incredible. Around two hundred million years ago, when the earth's land mass was one supercontinent, cracks appeared throughout the earth's crust which allowed molten lava to flow towards the surface and cool into soft, loosely joined basalt. The Batoka Gorge was formed as the Zambezi slowly, over millions of years, carved its way through this basalt. It was of course David Livingstone who was the first Westerner to view what the locals call *Mosi-oa-Tunya* (The Smoke That Thunders).

The experience moved him so much that he famously wrote in his journal: *on sights as beautiful as this, angels in their flight must have gazed*, and named them after his reigning monarch. So today, we all know this great waterfall as the Victoria Falls. The local beer is now called Mosi.

My dad loved taking photos. As we were walking along the opposite cliff edge, looking out at the awesome sight of the falls thundering down into the river, my dad decided this was the shot he wanted.

We had our backs to the cliff edge with the falls behind us when he said, "Just take a few steps back." I swore to him that there weren't any more steps to take and point-blank refused to move!

Our time in Zambia was the first moment I became aware that all was not well between my parents. When we were staying in Isoka I remember my mum locking herself in our bedroom. My dad was pounding at the door, shouting at my mum to let him in or else he would break the door down. The next day I remember getting into bed with my mum and dad, as my brother and I would often do. Everything seemed okay, but of course it wasn't.

My father decided that Zambia was no place for his kids to be educated. He said to my brother and I that the schools in Zambia were awful and that he wanted to send us to boarding school. The British government would help subsidise places for us, so it was a question of choosing where we would like to go. For some reason I wasn't really phased by the idea of going. My dad was a very convincing salesman and sold the idea to us with great gusto. I guess neither my brother nor I really understood the implications of living away from our parents. My dad presented us with a choice of two schools in Wolverhampton. One of my dad's reasons for choosing this particular city was that he had a friend who lived in Wolverhampton and another in Birmingham with whom we could stay during holidays. One option was a mixed school, and the other was all boys. Both of us went for the all-boys school – Tettenhall College.

It wasn't long before my brother and I were greeted at the airport by our aunt and uncle back in England, having flown across by ourselves, and we were soon making the trip up to Wolverhampton from London. Tettenhall College was to be our home for the next two years.

CHAPTER 4

BOARDING SCHOOL

While I didn't really notice or remember the absence of my mum and dad when I was in Pakistan during the first few years of my life, I certainly missed my parents when I went to boarding school.

When we arrived we were shown to our dorm on the top floor of the building where all the boys stayed. The older boys, aged thirteen years and above, slept in the dorms on the floor beneath us, and further downstairs was a canteen area. The dorm that my brother and I occupied for that first year housed around eight boys under the age of ten. We each had a bed and bedside table. There wasn't really any privacy. The bathroom facilities were shared and we had a TV room for chilling later in the day if we had time. There was also a games room which had table tennis and a few board games.

Tettenhall College itself was huge. It had a swimming pool, squash courts, tennis courts, four rugby pitches and woodland areas complete with a small cliff I remember abseiling down, supervised by one of our rock-climbing enthusiast teachers. To all intents and purposes, this was one of the best boarding schools in the UK.

The boarding school itself, where the full-time boarders slept, was an old Victorian house. It was three storeys high and very grand. All the interior was typically Victorian in style, very beautiful and with ornately carved wooden banisters and panelling. The younger boarders like me were on the top floor. The floors were all polished wood and I often got splinters in my feet if I forgot to wear my slippers. We had a TV room, which we were allowed to go to in the evenings once we had finished our homework.

Although I missed my parents immensely, I learned very quickly to be self-sufficient. There was an expectation that we were there to learn and do well. Standards were high. If you were a full-time boarder, you were expected to stay behind every evening after school for an hour to do your homework.

The lower school was for boys between the ages of ten and thirteen, around a five-minute walk from the building where the boarders lived. Some of the boys, in fact most of them, were considered to be day-boarders. They only attended the school during the day and then went home. I really wished I was one of those kids.

I was invited a couple of times to stay for a weekend at my friends' houses during what was called 'boarders' weekend'. It was when I went back to boarding school after one of those weekends that I used to get really homesick. On one particular occasion I was missing my parents so badly that I was in tears. The head teacher of the lower school and the man responsible for full-time boarders, Mr McCormack, saw me crying. Instead of putting his hand on my shoulder or giving me some words of comfort, he told me not to worry and that I would get over it. It dawned on me then that this was a cold and uncaring place, and as soon as I got the opportunity to leave, I would. I so wanted to go home.

It wasn't all bad though. The weekends were brilliant as I got plenty of free time to play and have fun. We got weekly pocket money of around £1 on Saturday mornings (money which was included in the school fees!). The money burnt a hole in my pocket until I ran down to the local village newsagent or mini supermarket to stock up on sweets and fizzy drinks. Oh yes, very unhealthy! The calories from the sugary goodies were soon burnt off playing war games in the woods, football or cricket, and if we were lucky, one of the teachers would open up the swimming pool for us to have an evening swim. I got copious amounts of exercise and fresh air!

While playing in the massive grounds of Tettenhall College, we would come across the very friendly school caretaker, a man in his forties wearing a tweed jacket and jeans. His daughter was in her early teens, very pretty and down-to-earth with her easy, relaxed manner, and would sometimes be hanging around on the weekends. She would often say hello and I would say hello back but had no idea how to carry on the conversation. The opposite sex were a bit of a mystery to me. Having lived at the boarding school for two years and been around boys all the time, I just had no idea how to behave around girls. The best policy, I thought, was to keep my mouth firmly closed, just in case I said something stupid.

The weekend soon came to an end. This was marked by the Sunday evening church service, which we had to attend. I really resented going to church as firstly, it wasn't my faith, and secondly (and more to the point), it was totally dull. There was only one service I remember enjoying where the man delivering the sermon was extremely entertaining, cracking a few jokes and using props to make his point. Apart from that – boring. One thing I do remember that touched me considerably was a plaque on the church wall which had a list of young men, around the age of 17, who had served in the Second World War and died. I was struck by the fact that these boys who had served their country were only a few years older than me. It did make me feel extremely sad to see their names on the wall.

During the holidays, my brother Toseef and I would spend a

few weeks either with my dad's friends in Wolverhampton or with his other friend in Birmingham. The family in Wolverhampton were my dad's old Sikh friends who my parents had lodged with before I was born. They looked after us well but I don't think that their boys, who were slightly younger than us, liked us being there. I became more and more reluctant to stay at their house. I really didn't feel welcome.

The other family in Birmingham were Muslim, and Mr Sheikh worked at the Cadbury's factory. That was pretty cool as he often brought home chocolate. Despite this, his kids were never fat! I got on well with his oldest lad, who was the same age as me. The younger brother was around five years old and a pain in the backside. Once, he swung his rather hard plastic cricket bat into my head for no particular reason. It really hurt, and unfortunately I decided to smack him in the face. Mr Sheikh wasn't very happy with me for doing that. I guess from the point of view of my dad's friends' wives it must have been a massive responsibility and possibly a burden to look after someone else's kids. It made me feel awful and made me even more homesick.

My eyesight problems seemed to be getting progressively worse. When I was eleven years old I noticed that I was struggling in dim light, whereas all my friends seemed to manage fine at night-time. When we walked back from school to the boarding house in the dark, I was having to rely upon any lights I could see along the five-minute trek. I used to dread any situation which took me into dim lighting. I also noticed that if I was going from light to dark, going indoors in the evening, for instance, it would take several minutes for my eyes to adjust. I was temporarily blind. This was really disconcerting, as no one else seemed to have any problems. When anyone asked me why I couldn't see properly I struggled to explain. The truth of the matter was I had no idea.

The other thing I noticed was that when I was playing football, the ball would sometimes disappear out of my field of vision. I would have to move my head around in order to scan the ground in front of me. When I first started school I was a pretty good footballer – small and nippy, always in the right place at the right time. I used to get picked first for the games we played during break time. However, as my eyesight deteriorated, so did my performance on the field and I was gradually bumped down the order and started getting picked last. This didn't help my self-confidence.

I know that Toseef was having similar problems. In fact cricket was becoming positively dangerous, as, during PE, we would play with a proper cricket ball. During one game, Toseef told me that his friend stuck his hand out to catch a ball which was flying straight at my brother's face. Toseef simply hadn't seen it.

Despite the eyesight problems I still managed to get some decent grades across the board, apart from French. I just didn't get French, probably not helped by the fact that most of the lessons were done using the blackboard, which I couldn't really see. A friend of mine once asked if he could borrow my French homework as he hadn't done his. He copied my homework to the letter. The usually mild-mannered French teacher went completely ballistic, and kept us both back for detention. I was extremely upset at the time as I felt that I was only trying to help out a mate. Lesson learned there.

Most of the teachers were quite good towards me, except my form teacher, Mr Swine. He was a nasty piece of work. I was pretty scared of upsetting him. When I was twelve years old I had him for geography lessons. He was a very good geography teacher, but it was his way of humiliating pupils he didn't like which I found cruel. One day I was the subject of his need to bully and it brought me to tears.

My hair was a little long and may have been over my eyes. He pointed to the only other Asian kid in the class and said, "Look, he doesn't have his hair covering his eyes!" He then pulled my hair back and put a bulldog clip in it, which actually was quite painful. Later that day Mr Swine saw me on the stairs going to my other classes and apologised. He looked really worried. Maybe he thought I would complain to my parents or the head. I don't know, but I didn't feel in a position to complain or tell anyone. I just wanted to forget about it.

My art teacher, on the other hand, was very impressed with my drawings and paintings. Despite my failing eyesight, I still had enough sight at this stage to be able to see things which were close to me and with strong contrasts. I was able to produce a good standard of artwork. I remember that in my last report I got over 80% for my landscape painting, which was practically unheard of.

During the last year of boarding school, I discovered that I had a talent for running. In 1982 I was picked to represent the school for the inter-school athletics competition in the eight hundred metres, even though I was better at the 1,500 metres. I was the smallest in the field, and when the gun went off all I remember is that all the other lads started to elbow and jostle for position (something I wasn't used to). In fact I was shocked at the aggressiveness of my fellow runners.

When I got back to school my friends asked me how I did. I told them that I had come fifth, and they congratulated me for doing so well. I pointed out to them that I was fifth out of six! Being the true friends they were, they said, "Still, that's good, Haseeb." That certainly made me feel so much better – after all, it was the first proper out-of-school competition I had taken part in.

In the same year, I won the sports day 1,500 metres race. I heard one of the teachers say after I crossed the line, "I didn't know Haseeb was good at running." Yes, and I won in a pair of Dunlop tennis shoes!

In many ways Tettenhall College was good for me. Yes, I didn't have my parents around and it was tough at times, but the education was brilliant. I learned a great deal and, of course, I found out I was good at a number of things, including running. The two years of high-quality education were very important in terms of helping me through the next few years of my life which involved changing schools and coping with my rapidly deteriorating eyesight.

CHAPTER 5

BACK IN THE BIG SMOKE

On one of his visits to the UK from Zambia, in the spring of 1982, my father asked my brother and me if we wanted to carry on at boarding school. We both wanted Mum and Dad to come back to the UK and for us to live together in our family home in London. To my surprise, Dad allowed my mum to travel back to England, from Zambia during the summer – he still had another year to go on his contract.

Toseef and I got on the coach from Wolverhampton at the end of the summer term and were met by Mum at Victoria coach station, London. When we got off, she asked us how we would feel about having another brother or sister. Well, I was fast approaching twelve years old and I couldn't believe that my mum was going to have another baby. I actually remember saying to her that she was lying, but once the reality had sunk in, I was so excited. I actually wanted a baby sister, and I know my mum wanted a girl. Whatever the outcome, it was lovely to think we were going to have a new addition to the family.

For the next few months we lived in a small room in my Auntie Kaneez's house in Streatham, as our family house was being rented to students for another year. My brother, my pregnant mum and I all slept together in a double bed. I really don't know how we did it, looking back. It was a very stressful time for my mum. She was always worried that my brother and

I would be a nuisance to my aunt and uncle, so tried to keep us cooped up in the room. These weren't happy times.

It was during this time that we started our new school, Dick Sheppard School in Brixton. Compared to what we were used to this was a godawful place. As we had been to a private boarding school, my dad had somehow managed to get my brother and me a year ahead of the school year we should have been in. So, I ended up being the youngest by far in my year – Year 3 (now Year 9). The contrast between the schools couldn't have been more apparent. A real culture shock. I was utterly stunned at the lack of discipline at Dick Sheppard. Often the classes were unruly, and the teachers were simply unable to control them. Those kids who wanted to learn had to fend for themselves. I hated it.

Once a teacher decided to give the whole class detention at the end of the school day. He stood at the door to ensure that no one left the class. I was fifteen years old at this time and so the rest of the class were around sixteen years old. One of the kids, a very fit, tall and well-built Caribbean lad, took umbrage at being held back from going home at the end of the school day and took matters into his own hands. He picked up the teacher and practically threw him to one side. The teacher was a young white man and probably in his mid twenties, so no lightweight. I was really astounded by what had just happened. A few days later I heard the kid had been expelled.

On a lighter note, I remember being taught by a supply teacher who said he was an actor. On being further interrogated by the class he told us that he was going to feature in a new comedy based in France during the Second World War. It was going to be called 'Allo 'Allo! and he was one of the English airmen the French Resistance went to great lengths to hide. I can tell you that his acting skills were far better than his teaching. In his case it was a good decision to give up the day job!

During the mid 1980s, my eyesight continued to get worse. I was not able to see the blackboard and struggled to cope in crowded situations where the lighting was poor. Trying to walk down busy school corridors and not bump into other pupils was an increasing challenge. Going into a dimly lit classroom was a nightmare as my eyes adjusted very slowly, not allowing me to make out chairs and tables. It was just so stressful. It became a real issue. I began to avoid going to lunch, which was served in a couple of the bigger classrooms, instead opting to buy a hotdog from the ice cream van that stopped at the school gates. By the time I walked home to Streatham (around two miles), I was so hungry I had to pop into a newsagent to buy myself a packet of treats (M&Ms). I couldn't wait for dinner to be served. Needless to say, I was very skinny. Obesity wasn't going to be an issue for me.

My terrible eyesight had a fundamental impact on my confidence levels. My ability to move around easily and notice the finer detail of what was going on even at close proximity was seriously impaired. I was a sensitive and self-conscious soul, which didn't help matters. This was further compounded by the fact that my father insisted that my brother and I, having studied at private school, were to be put in the year group above the one we ordinarily would have been placed in. So, all the other kids in my year were a year older than me. On my first day at school some girls in the same form as me, being fascinated with the new kid on the block, started asking me lots of questions like, "Where did you go to school before? Where do you live?" and so on. I was so shy and self-conscious that I kept my answers to single words and just looked down. This is in contrast to the person I am now. I think that if it wasn't for my awful sight impairment at the time I would have really enjoyed the school experience, even if the school I was at post-1982 was an educational disaster zone.

My terrible eyesight was also a hindrance in the girlfriend

department. I remember one particular incident when I was in a design and technology lesson working on one of my projects, and a girl came into the room and stood next to me.

"My friend over there fancies you."

I didn't dare look up. I knew that if I tried to scan around for her the chances were that I wouldn't be able to spot her friend. Now I like to think that if I had been able to see her I wouldn't have been interested. But it would have been nice to have the choice!

However, back then I have to say I felt very alone and really didn't feel as though I had anyone I could talk to. It would have been nice to have had a special girlfriend I could share my worries with. A few years later, when I did have a girlfriend when I was in the sixth form, I did share the fact that I couldn't see properly. It didn't seem to bother her but I don't think either she or I understood the full implications of my blindness.

During 1982, on top of the struggle I was having with my undiagnosed blindness, I experienced a nasty racist attack on my way home from school. It was like any other day and Toseef and I were messing around, pushing each other and laughing.

We were practically around the corner from my aunt's house when two teenagers on a bike went by, and one shouted, "You stupid Pakis!"

Without thinking, I turned around and told him to "Shut up."

As we turned the corner onto Salford Road the two lads turned around and followed us up the road. They stopped us and one of the boys got off the bike and hit me over the head with a bag containing a hard object. It hurt, and I started crying. The lad told me never to talk back to him. He then grabbed my metal-rimmed glasses off my face and bent them in half.

The older lad of the two, who was piloting the bike, then intervened, saying, "Hey, don't break his glasses. I mean, you can hit him, but don't break them." He took the glasses and bent them back into shape! How kind.

There is no doubt in my mind that this was a racist attack, totally unprovoked. I felt so angry and ashamed. There was no reason to feel ashamed but, when you experience an attack of this sort, all of a sudden you have no control over what is happening to you. I felt powerless at the time and powerless afterwards. I didn't tell anyone, and was frightened for quite some time afterwards that it would happen again. In fact, a couple of years later I took the opportunity to learn martial arts when lessons were given at the local mosque. I wanted to be able to defend myself if ever it was to happen again.

Back at school, I soon made friends with a lad from Green House called Martyn McKenna. Martyn was to become very important in my life over the next couple of years. He was a fairly quiet and sensitive boy, a bit like myself, and different, which made him a target for bullying by some of the other kids. Martyn was also very good at art, something which I really admired, and we shared the same taste in music. I hung out with Martyn a lot. This had the unfortunate consequence of other kids insinuating we were gay.

There is nothing wrong with being gay of course, but I wasn't. What made things even worse was that around this time, my friends in Red House stopped talking to me. One of the boys told the other lads to stop communicating with Martyn and me. I really couldn't understand why. I asked all the boys concerned what the problem was and why they weren't talking to me any more, but none of them would offer an explanation. Weird. So, I confronted the ringleader one day outside the school library and we got into a fight. The boy I was fighting with came off worse. During the fight my glasses had come off my face and one of the boys watching stepped on them and smashed one of the lenses – collateral damage, I guess. A teacher came along and broke us up, and I sat through the afternoon's classes with even less sight than usual and sore knuckles. I have to say that all the bullying stopped. But I was still unhappy at school, and my home life wasn't great either.

My brother Shazib was born on the 13th December 1982, shortly after we moved back into our family home on Leander Road. This was a mid-terraced Victorian house, three storeys high with four bedrooms and two large reception rooms. I loved it for its size, and my parents had done a grand job upgrading it. However, all was not well. My father was still in Zambia and my brother and I had to go out and do the shopping while my mum was at home looking after Shazib. My mum wasn't coping well. It was obvious that she wasn't happy. My baby brother was a delight. I was so happy that he had arrived. I remember how cute and beautiful he was. I used to hold him as often as I could and I remember chatting to him regularly, telling him my worries and problems, although he didn't understand a word I was telling him – well, hopefully not!

Shazib's thoughts and memories, in his own words:

I always knew that my older brothers had some form of health issues. My dad constantly took my younger brother, Tahseen, and me to have our eyes checked, and I did sometimes get the impression that he saw my older brothers as flawed. But they took me to the park all the time when my mum and dad could not, they played games with me, made me laugh, made sure I did not kill Tahseen, my little brother, by sticking his head down the toilet to wash it (hey, I was three), in Haseeb's case played the guitar and drums, got A Levels and were going off to university – to me they were heroes.

Haseeb going to university was one of the most difficult times in my life – I had never spent so long away from him before. The one who gave me advice on how to deal with bullies, how to be proud of who I am, to never give up, was no longer just upstairs in his bedroom. He called on a regular basis, but I missed him immensely. But at least he visited us, or I got to go and visit him with my younger brother in Leicester. So it wasn't so bad.

Then, when I was eleven, my dad took my younger brother and me to Pakistan. Promises of a green and pleasant land were made, but never did materialise. Now, more than ever, I needed my big brother. He phoned on a regular basis – I now realise that it must have cost him a fortune, as at the time, phone cards were not around; it was at BT's international rates, and I would hate to think what sacrifices he would have had to make, all just to call and check we were okay.

I remember the call from Haseeb to tell me that Mary, his wife, was pregnant; the call to say that Ayeisha had been born – all moments I missed out on. But my view of my brother as a family man was being laid down. The man who would sacrifice to make sure his family was okay.

When I came back to Britain (and what a relief!), during the summer holidays of 1998, I spent some time staying with Haseeb and his family. Over the years I had come to understand what retinitis pigmentosa was – but I also saw how it didn't keep my brother from living a fuller and more productive life than most of us ever will. He had a career, a family, a brilliant sense of humour and was wise beyond his years.

I had a slightly warped view of the world, I will admit – my father's view. My brother challenged it, taught me to always keep an open mind, respect other people's opinions whilst staying true to my own and to treat everyone equally and fairly. I owe a lot of my character to him.

In more recent years Haseeb has rediscovered his passion for sports. He has won medals at an international level and most recently broken the world record for completing an Ironman Triathlon blindfolded (although completely blind the Guinness

Book of Records state that Haseeb had to do it blind-folded).

So, we are talking about a man with a disability who has gone on to achieve more than most non-disabled people do in an entire lifetime. A man who has inspired me, taught me life lessons, someone who I still aspire to emulate.

Haseeb Ahmad – you are an amazing man, and I am proud to call you my brother.

In 1983 my father's contract in Zambia came to an end and he returned home. Meanwhile, my mum's mental health worsened. She eventually ended up in a psychiatric hospital, having been diagnosed with postnatal depression. She was in hospital for what seemed like months, but it might have been weeks. When we visited her she seemed really sad, I mean, just totally out of it. My mum is usually a very chatty and expressive person. She would constantly tell us stories of her childhood, or tell us off for misbehaving as we were growing up. It was strange seeing her so down and unable to communicate. I think some of it may have been the medication, but mostly it was the nature of the condition. What made me really unhappy was the fact that Shazib was in hospital with her. I just wanted them back home.

Around this time my dad asked my grandparents to come from Pakistan to look after my brother and me. It wasn't long before my mum and Shaz were back home. However, coping with day-to-day life continued to be a massive challenge for me as my sight got worse and there were no answers as to why this was happening to me.

CHAPTER 6

MUSIC, COMICS AND ATARI GAMES

Life at school went from bad to worse while I was ostracised from most of my friends, and I was finding it difficult to cope at school due to my rapidly failing eyesight. I used to call for Martyn and we would walk to school together. One day when I knocked on Martyn's front door, his mum told me that he wasn't going to school, and asked me whether I wanted to come in. I stepped into the flat and found to my surprise that Martyn wasn't ill. In fact, he seemed in great health. I asked him why he wasn't going in, and his answer was simply that he didn't feel like it. I could see his point. The school was rubbish, we weren't learning anything and we got bullied on a daily basis, so what was the point?

I did intend to go to school that day, but ended up staying at his flat all day. Martyn's mum was at home and she knew we weren't going in. She didn't seem to mind. Actually, I think she was pretty glad that I was keeping Martyn company.

Martyn was the youngest of three boys. His two brothers were much older than him; one was a lighthouse keeper and the other, believe it or not, was a surgeon. Both had studied at The Strand, which was the local grammar school before it was merged with Dick Sheppard under the new comprehensive schooling system. So it seemed bizarre to me when his brothers had done so well that Martyn's parents appeared to sanction his boycott of the education system. On the other hand, for Martyn and me it was certainly preferable to the day-to-day ordeal we were subjected to in attending a substandard school where we felt marginalised. I really did feel safe at Martyn's flat.

One day turned into another of spending time at Martyn's flat instead of school. We would either read comics (Martyn introduced me to *2000 AD* and *Judge Dredd* – he was really good at art and I quite liked the artwork in the comics), listen to music such as Iron Maiden and Metallica, watch a film or play computer games. Much easier than going to school.

As the length of time spent truanting increased, I felt more and more guilty, and wondered when I would be caught. The fact that I wasn't found out for some considerable time was due to my form tutor (responsible for taking the register) regularly being on sick leave. He was a nice guy, Mr Zenetti.

I would turn up to school every now and again and Mr Zenetti would ask, "Haseeb, have you been in school for the last few days?"

Of course I would say, "Yes, sir." I hadn't been in at all! It was only a matter of time until someone noticed I was missing from classes. The longer it went on, the more worried I got that I would finally be caught.

It took around two years before the school discovered my frequent absences. I remember it well. Mrs O'Flaherty, who was the head of Yellow House, called me to her office. She was pretty good with me really. She asked me whether I had been skipping school. I owned up, and she said it was up to me whether the school or I told my parents.

That day I went home and confessed all to my dad. I really expected a good beating from him. Although I was scared of my father, he didn't often hit me. It was only on the rare occasion if I had overstepped the mark. On this occasion, he became extremely tearful and started to cry. I felt so bad, and I was also crying. I was really sorry for what I had done, but clearly couldn't undo it. All I could do was go back to school and try to salvage my education.

My father had such high expectations of Toseef and me. I knew that I had just let him down big time, but I couldn't undo what had happened. However, this was an opportunity for me to make a clean break from Martyn. Although at the beginning of our friendship I enjoyed Martyn's company and his parent's flat was a safe place to go, tension started to creep into our relationship. Deep down I knew our friendship wasn't entirely positive. He started to put me down, saying that I wasn't much good at anything. My love of art meant that despite my poor eyesight I still enjoyed drawing and painting, but Martyn would be extremely disparaging about my artwork. I was kind of glad that I wasn't going to see him any more, and to be going back to school, as scary as the prospect seemed.

On 23rd July 1984, when I was fourteen, my youngest brother Tahseen was born. I remember when I first found out that my mum was expecting again, I exclaimed how mad it was that she was having another baby, considering what happened after Shaz was born. Inevitably, after Tahseen was born, my mum ended up back in the psychiatric hospital again. Our parents told us the reason for having another child was to give Shaz a brother to play with. Shazib was around eighteen months old and just about walking when Tahseen came home. Initially, Shaz was very jealous of all the attention focused on his baby brother. Needless to say, Tahseen was lovely, and it was fantastic having two baby brothers in tow. Well, most of the time. I did love taking them down to the park and playing with them on a regular basis. As the older two brothers, Toseef and I would help our younger brothers with their homework, reading and writing, and it was so rewarding as my younger brothers were bright little things.

For my mum, however, it was hard going. My dad had decided not to go back to teaching and bought a shop practically up the road from us, and the hours were very long. He did his very best to run the shop and give all of us as much support as he could, but it was difficult. When he was a teacher it seemed as though my dad was at home most of the time. He'd spend a great deal of time with Toseef and me, getting us to practise our times tables or spelling. He was pretty strict and I remember being really scared of him, particularly if I got my times tables wrong. But I also remember how much I loved him as a young child. As a teenager, though, my feelings towards him had hardened somewhat. There were times I really hated him – nothing unusual there, then!

When my dad bought the shop, an off-licence, he did so in partnership with my uncle. It was in fact two shops, but at the time only the off-licence was open and the other shop was used for storage. We used to be able to pop into the shop and pick up some sweets, ice cream or hair gel, as I often did, but I was always careful not to take advantage of the ability to go in after school and help myself to everything on offer.

Going back to school after I was caught truanting was tough, but actually, I felt a sense of relief. I could now concentrate on my studies and try to salvage some qualifications. I soon became friendly with another boy called Enver, who was of Greek Cypriot origin. He was also very artistic and into thrash metal. We went to a few gigs together. My first ever gig was to see a band called Slayer, on their debut tour in England, at the old Marquee. I was only fifteen and was surprised that my dad let me go. When we went into the venue I remember not being able to see anything. The place smelt weird and I got pinned against the front barriers near to the stage. I was right over a speaker and got absolutely deafened during the performance. A skinhead decided to stage-dive but, unfortunately for him, instead of catching the bloke everyone just moved out of the way and he landed on his head. It was a great gig. I saw Slayer again a couple of years later at the Hammersmith Odeon, a much more civilised affair as it was all seated and there was no mosh pit.

Back at school, I still don't know how I was managing. The classes were still chaotic with very little discipline. A couple of teachers were having nervous breakdowns. During one lesson, my geography teacher started telling us about his relationship problems with his son and got very tearful. I felt really sorry for him, but it wasn't the kind of school where you could show any sort of weakness in front of the kids. The history teacher once ran out in a flood of tears and refused to go back and teach the class. In light of this and the very unsupportive school culture I didn't feel I had anyone I could confide in regarding my terrible eyesight problems. I had no choice but to get my head down and do my best with the little sight I had. I was able to read with a book close up to my face, and I was still able to make out my own handwriting. On reflection, I really don't know how I survived, but survive I did. I guess you either get on with life or give up. It wasn't in my nature to just throw the towel in.

I think the two years of private education I got saw me through my first set of exams in 1986. I was a year ahead and managed to get two O Levels in art and English. My dad wasn't very happy of course and, inevitably, I had to stay on to take some more O Levels in the sixth form.

For me, to be perfectly honest, it was a good result, all things considered. Yet, I couldn't explain to my father that my poor results were a direct consequence of my blindness. I never, ever used that terminology when I tried to explain to my dad that I couldn't see very well. It never entered my head that I was going blind. The whole concept of being blind or partially sighted was alien to me. Yet, I had already worked out that there was something very wrong with my vision, and that it could be something to do with my field of vision. Once I had tried to explain to my friend Martyn that it was like having several blind spots when I was trying to look around.

I never saw Martyn again. I realise that the relationship was an unhealthy one. We had been thrown together as a result of circumstances, we were both unhappy and it suited us to hang around together. But we wanted different things in life. I really wanted to go back to school and do well. It was just that I couldn't cope in the school environment without a considerable amount of stress. Now, I had no choice but to go back to school and soldier on.

Going back to school full-time had the consequence of allowing me to make more friends. This was towards the end of 1985. I hung around with two lads, Mark Saunders and Matthew Walkling, quite a bit, and also became friendly with an Afro-Caribbean lad called Richard Stevens. These were the same boys who had stopped talking to me a couple of years ago, but all of that seemed to be behind us now.

Mark and I started hanging out after school. He was such a happy-go-lucky guy and had loads of confidence (the very opposite to me). He was pretty chatty and always had something to say or an opinion to offer. He was good-looking and charming. Everything I wanted to be, but wasn't! I couldn't understand why he wanted to hang out with me, but I wasn't complaining. He was cool to be with. Years later, Mark told me that in fact he found me to be really interesting and engaging. I was different, and he quite liked that about me.

One afternoon at school, when waiting to get into the swimming pool changing rooms, we were hanging around outside the pool building. Behind us was Brockwell Park, and the only thing separating the school from the park was a metal fence. Behind the fence were a couple of Caribbean boys, probably a year younger than me. They started calling me names, including some racist names. You would have thought I would have learned from my last experience of racism, and ignored the taunts. Instead I started hurling back the abuse. The boys disappeared and my friends and I went in for our swim.

After coming out from the pool, we were making our way back into the main building when these lads reappeared. One of them (the smaller of the two) started pushing me around and it wasn't long before we were exchanging blows. I had started to smash the boy against a wall when a teacher came along to spoil my fun. The lads didn't belong to the school and, as I turned my back, the other boy came at me with a massive wooden stick. Mark shouted at me and I just managed to dodge a blow from it. The lads ran off. I later heard that the boys were waiting for me at one of the school gates with their friends, but I had left the school using another exit so managed to escape unscathed.

According to one of the boys in my year, the lad I was fighting was a notorious gang member called 'Yellow Baby'. The boy telling me this said, "You were lucky that he didn't wet you." I thought this an odd comment, and must have looked a little confused. He clarified things: "You're lucky he didn't knife you, man."

CHAPTER 7

SIXTH FORM YEARS AND DIAGNOSIS

School in 1985 was a matter of plodding along and trying to do what I could to get through my O Levels (if I was allowed to take them) or my CSEs (which were the exams you took if you weren't deemed bright enough to do O Levels). I quite enjoyed English language, wasn't bad at art, despite being half blind, and still had a flair for maths. Design and technology was tricky, though. In one D&T lesson a classmate decided to point the blowtorch in my direction as I was turned away from him, but fortunately for me the flame didn't quite reach my backside!

It wasn't long before it was exam time, and once they were over I had no idea how I had done. Was I going to come away with some reasonable qualifications with which to go on to do something useful, or was I going to fail spectacularly?

While I waited for the results during the summer of 1986 I hung out with my good friend Mark Saunders. Mark had already decided that he wasn't going to stay at school and was going to find himself a job. He was just so incredibly confident that I didn't doubt it for a second. However, in the meantime there was fun to be had!

Mark suggested, on one very hot day sometime in July, that we should take a trip down to Regent's Park and find ourselves some girlfriends.

"Okay," I recall saying, but thought this a rather pointless exercise. My confidence around girls was pretty much zero at this time. I didn't know where to start.

However, on reaching Regent's Park we strolled through the beautifully manicured lawns. Mark had his shirt wide open and to my amazement, a number of girls were wolf-whistling. My jealousy reached another level. Eventually we came across a group of girls on a school trip. They were a year below us, but took great interest in Mark. One of them quite fancied him and gave him her number. I came away empty-handed as usual. Well, looking back I am not at all surprised. I didn't have much dress sense and wasn't gifted in the chat-up line department. Mark on the other hand was extremely chatty and outgoing and seemed so at ease with himself. Years later I was to be reunited with my old friend and found out that all was not as it seemed.

The summer days passed by and felt like they would never end. Sometimes we would pop down to the Crystal Palace swimming pool. This was the only fifty-metre pool in London at the time, and had a ten-metre diving board. I remember standing on the top diving board and looking down. Mark dared me to jump off. I didn't have my glasses on (so was practically blind), and when I dared to peer over the diving board, I couldn't even see the pool below! Needless to say, I didn't jump off.

When it was time to pick up my results the nerves kicked in. I remember walking down to the school, and in those days the results were pinned up on a board for all to see. I had to stand very close to the results sheet to see what I had got. I got a C in English language, E in English lit, B in art (wow), Level 2 in CSE maths and pretty much flunked everything else. Well, it was enough to stay on for sixth form and do some more O Levels. My dad insisted that I retake English, so I did as I was told even though I thought it pointless. I mean, I had passed already so why go through it all again? Anyway, I decided to take history, geography, maths and accounting at CSE level.

I really enjoyed going back to school as a sixth-former. The classes were smaller and most of the kids who stayed on were serious about gaining some additional qualifications. In the previous year I don't think there were many who got more than a couple of passes in their GCEs. There was only one boy, Adrian, who wore a hearing aid and was very studious; he got five GCE passes and left to go to college to do his A Levels. Yes, that pass rate confirmed to me that this was indeed a pretty sub-standard school. However, I couldn't leave as I was still fifteen years old and so legally I had to stay on.

But that was okay as I needed to get some more O Levels in order to go on to do my A Levels, which would then get me into university. Well, that was the plan. I wasn't sure at this time what I wanted to do as a career in the future. In fact, the future terrified me. I knew my eyesight was terrible and just couldn't think what I would do for a job. The future seemed bleak. If I was struggling at school and in my day-to-day life, how on earth was I going to cope in a job? Who would employ me when I couldn't see much further than my nose? I really tried not to think about it too much, because when I did I just felt so down. My father had such high expectations of my brother and me, and I didn't want to let him down. I knew I wasn't lacking intelligence; I had a great memory and at boarding school I had done extremely well. I really didn't know what to do or who to turn to.

I knew that I couldn't do anything practical work-wise. When I was around fifteen years old I tried a little stint working at my dad's shop. He gave me £5 a week to stand in the corner of the shop to ensure that no one was shoplifting. Unfortunately, my dad had spotted someone taking a bottle of spirits and tucking it into his jacket. This had happened right under my nose. Well, I realised there and then that there was no future for me in shop-floor security!

So, I stayed on at lower sixth form and went on to do a few

more subjects during 1985–1986 and took some more O Levels in the summer of 1986. It was during this year that I got to know Chris Snuggs, who was going to Tulse Hill School. The sixth form was made up of students from three of the local schools: Dick Sheppard, which was a mixed-intake school, Tulse Hill, a comprehensive for boys, and St Martin's, a comprehensive school for girls. Chris was really good fun and was interested in music. The previous year I had started learning to play the drums, and I was really happy to meet someone who not only shared my interest in music, but wanted to start up a band. So, Chris, my brother and I started to rehearse above one of my dad's shops. We got lots of complaints from the neighbours, who thought we were too loud, so we endeavoured to find a music teacher at Tulse Hill School who then allowed us to practise in the music room. He even joined us on one occasion on his guitar; it was so much fun even though we were pretty bad.

This was also the year that I applied my finely honed chess skills I had acquired as a young child. There was a group of boys I hung out with who decided to run a mini chess tournament. We would all put in £1 and battle against each other in a head-to-head contest. The winner took all, and that was normally me. My competitive instincts kicked in; I just couldn't help it – a theme that would return later in my life as a runner and triathlete.

After my exams during that summer of 1986, my brother, Chris and I, through the help of the music teacher, got a two-week placement at a music school. This was a fantastic experience and we had loads of fun rehearsing and recording some tunes. During the two-week period it was obvious that Toseef and I were struggling to get around as our sight continued to deteriorate. Going from light to dimly-lit areas was getting to be a challenge to say the least. It was impossible to explain to others why I couldn't see properly. It was just so incredibly frustrating. My friend Chris was finding it difficult to understand that Toseef and I needed help when it got dark at night, or in situations of low lighting due to the night-blindness effect of the eye condition. I think that my friends thought it was all a bit weird, or maybe they thought Toseef and I were making it all up.

Towards the end of 1986 my exam results finally arrived. I didn't do too badly, as far as I was concerned. I got what I needed to do some A Levels, but naturally my dad wasn't happy that I didn't get straight As. Not an unusual response from an Asian dad! I really didn't care. My dad had no idea what I was going through and how hard I had to work to get those grades. He didn't have a clue that the reading and writing I was doing was putting additional stress on my failing eyes. He didn't have a clue about the headaches and stress I was suffering on a day-to-day basis. He didn't have a clue because I never told him. I didn't feel I could talk to him like a friend. We just don't consider our parents to be 'mates' within the Asian culture. We respect our parents, we don't answer back and we certainly don't do anything that goes against the community standards.

I so wanted my dad to be proud of me. I knew that I couldn't study medicine, so thought that I might have a go at studying accountancy at university. The subjects weren't available at my school, so, with my GCEs in hand, I decided to leave school to go to South London College to study economics, maths and statistics. This was, as I was to find out very quickly, a big mistake! Considering that all these subjects required a great deal of blackboard study and visual work, it was inevitable that I was going to struggle. Also, my blindness was becoming a real hindrance in terms of my mobility. I could get to the college, and once there, just about manage to get myself to classes, but it was getting increasingly difficult and this was compounded by my inability to recognise people unless they were reasonably close.

Making friends was therefore tricky. The other factor that made it difficult for me was the large number of students at the college, which I found overwhelming. I didn't last long. I was there a couple of months and decided that I would go back to school – if they would have me back, that is.

I approached Dick Sheppard School, who kindly took me back, and I decided to continue to try and study maths and economics, and take up sociology. I had to drop maths in the end despite the teacher's valiant attempts to provide me with additional tutoring to bring me up to the required standard. I just couldn't see anything he was doing on the blackboard, or even on a piece of paper when having one-to-one lessons with him. I didn't mind though; doing two A Levels was going to be a more manageable prospect than three.

I coped the best I could under the circumstances. The classes weren't too bad and sociology was a pretty cool subject that I could get my head around relatively easily. The sociology teacher was a really nice guy who was also a good laugh. I made some great friends, as the class sizes were very small. There was a lovely and kind Nigerian girl called Caroline. She had a couple of friends she hung out with, Catherine and Lorraine. I spent a lot of time chilling out with the girls up in the sixth form common room; they were very good fun. I was still good friends with Chris and we continued to play in the band.

It was during 1988, in my second year of A Levels, when I was seventeen and being driven somewhere in my dad's car, that Dad suggested that it might be a good idea if I started to have driving lessons now that I was seventeen. I wasn't sure how to respond, but thought honesty was the best policy, rather than trying to take up driving lessons and causing an RTA. So I told him that there was no way that I would be able to drive. I just couldn't see anything through the window as the sunshine dazzled my vision and my eyes were not adjusting to the glare of the sun.

My dad seemed to accept this. I think deep down he knew my eyesight was extremely poor. I guess we were all in denial. I don't know whether this was what prompted him to make an appointment with a qualified ophthalmologist on Streatham High Street for my brother and me. When we went for our appointment, the ophthalmologist ran some routine tests, which took around half an hour, after which he concluded that he suspected we had a condition called retinitis pigmentosa (RP). He said that the bad news was that if this was the condition, there was no cure. It's difficult to describe what I felt. It was a feeling of utter relief that at long last there was a reason for the sight loss. At long last I could tell my friends and family that my short-sightedness and lack of vision were a result of an eye disease for which there was no cure. I don't think the full impact of the diagnosis had quite sunk in.

The ophthalmologist referred us to St Thomas' Hospital for further tests. We had these in the winter of 1987 and both of us were registered blind straight away. The eye consultants at St Thomas' told us that the condition would stabilise and we shouldn't lose any more of our eyesight. How wrong they were.

Post-diagnosis, life went on. Both of us were continuing with our education. The first person I told at school was my sociology teacher, Mr Jones. He was such a cool teacher and I got on with him really well. He was also my form tutor, so I trusted him. I just remember asking him if I could have a private word with him. I didn't know quite what to say, so I got straight to the point.

"Mr Jones, I've been to the hospital about my eyes and they've told me I'm going blind."

He was utterly shocked and said how sorry he was. Once the diagnosis had been confirmed I got a lot more help at school. Mr Jones photocopied all the books and articles in a larger font, which was a great help, and I got help from the RNIB and was given a small loan to buy a typewriter. I learned to touch-type and Toseef and I also went for lessons in Braille. One of the things I couldn't quite get myself to do was to start using the white cane. My eyesight was bad by now and I was beginning to bump into things. I had to really scan the terrain in front of me to ensure that I didn't walk into anyone or anything.

It wasn't until I left school that I started to use a symbol cane just to inform people that I was partially sighted. There were two incidents that occurred on Streatham High Street which compelled me to start using the cane. Once I walked straight into some guy who was well over six foot tall and built like a brick outhouse. I didn't see him walking out of a shop and smacked straight into him. He waved his fist at me and I cowered, but fortunately, he didn't take a swing at me. The other incident was when I accidently kneed a toddler in the head because I didn't see her. Her mum gave me quite a bit of abuse, telling me to look where I was going! It's the hardest thing having to carry a white cane for the first time. The main reason is the stigma and embarrassment factor, and also it's the reality of having to admit to the world that you are visually impaired. It sets you apart from everyone else; people who have known you before or seen you at school or in the neighbourhood walking around as a sighted person one day, and then the next day they spot you carrying a white cane.

There were quite a few occasions when kids who recognised me from school would say, "You're not blind – why are you carrying that stick?" This made me feel really angry on the one hand that my integrity was being questioned – I mean, why would I make up having a visual impairment? And on the other hand I felt vulnerable because if these boys decided to attack me I would have struggled to defend myself.

Nonetheless, I knew I had to rise above such taunts and negative challenges. I had to get my head down and work hard towards passing my A Levels, which was going to be easier said than done. I was still struggling to read, so I approached one of my friends to read on tape for me. My friend happened to be a Jehovah's Witness and he reluctantly agreed to read a couple of essays I had written on audio tape. He was reluctant mainly because his father questioned the content of the essay and thought his son might somehow be reading anti-religious propaganda and be somehow brain-washed! This was quite an unexpected opposition to something I felt was a reasonable request from a mate to help me in my studies.

The summer of 1988 soon arrived and it was exam time, *again*. I took my A Levels in June. I didn't really know what to expect, but I wasn't anticipating good grades. I had applied to do economics at university, which in hindsight was rather ambitious given the nature and content of the subject area. The results I got (B in sociology and E in economics) got me into Leicester Polytechnic. I was really nervous about going away to university, particularly regarding making friends, and talked this over with the social workers who had been teaching Toseef and me Braille and mobility. John Osbourne, our Braille teacher, was so nice, and he assured me that I would make friends easily. Those people who were naturally caring and kind, he said, would just become friends and be a great source of support. It did settle my nerves massively.

The end of September meant packing for Leicester Polytechnic. I was both excited and very anxious. What would the course be like, and would I make friends? How would I cope with my blindness on the course and in the halls of residence? I had lived away from home before at boarding school, but I had a great deal more sight in those days so was just able to cope. This was a real journey into the unknown. I was about to start afresh in a new city among people who didn't know me. The first impression they would get would be of this blind guy wandering around with his white cane. Would I really make friends or would fellow students avoid me? I was about to find out.

CHAPTER 8

UNIVERSITY YEARS

My dad dropped me off at Leicester Polytechnic – once we found it. These were the days before satnav, of course! I was staying at William Rowlett Halls somewhere off Narborough Road. The room I had was a ground-floor student bedroom with a sink. It looked really nice, by all accounts. The doors were a bit flimsy and I found out later in the term that some of the guys had punched holes through their doors, apparently in a fit of rage, no doubt fuelled by alcohol.

I need not have worried about making friends. The warden in charge of the halls of residence introduced me to a couple of students and asked them to take care of me. I recall one guy I was introduced to commenting that he had seen me walking around with my white cane which he mistook for a rubbish picking device! Another of these students was on my course and her name was Tracy. She was really sweet and very supportive. I also got to know a Caribbean guy on the same corridor as me called Owayne. Owayne often just walked into my room for a chat. I could just about make out people's features at very close quarters and recall that he was a handsome dude: tall, athletic and with a great smile. But I also knew that he was struggling with his own issues. He came from a strong Christian background and I could tell he was missing home. Like the rest of us, he was out of his comfort zone. He was also the only black guy in our halls of residence. I think he found me easy to talk to and I was always glad to see him. He told me once that he had shoplifted when he was younger, not that long before he came to university; however, he felt so bad and guilt-ridden that he went back to the shops where he had shoplifted and either paid for the stolen goods or took them back. He said that the shopkeepers thought him mad. I thought it was an extremely brave thing to do.

The other good friend I had who helped me out considerably was David, who was studying information technology. David would help me get to town to do shopping and we would go swimming on a regular basis. The thing I really remember, though, was the fact that while I was at Leicester Poly I was always reliant upon others to get me around. It was only in the halls of residence that I dared walk around by myself; otherwise I was always accompanied by one of my friends. My eyesight had got even worse and I was now struggling to read and write. I couldn't really get around by myself very well. Unfortunately for me, the campus was spread out somewhat and there was always a trek to various buildings for my lectures. I found the whole campus confusing to get around and crossing busy roads extremely scary. I knew my friends were getting frustrated that they had to walk me to lectures and tutorials that they didn't have to attend, and I too felt incredibly guilty and down because I couldn't be more independent. But as the weeks wore on I realised that I wasn't coping at all well with the course, despite a couple of good marks in some subject areas.

However, I tried to mask the fact that I was struggling with the course by partying hard. I would often resort to going out to clubs or pubs with friends and drinking more than I should have, although it didn't take a lot to get me drunk back then (or even now!). It became obvious to me (and probably those around me) that I wasn't going to last very long on the university course.

I spoke to a couple of the lecturers to explain that I wasn't coping; however they really wanted me to keep going. One of the economics lecturers even provided me with additional tuition. Again, I couldn't really see what he was trying to tutor me on, even though he used a thick black felt-tip pen on white paper to try and demonstrate economic theory and concepts. It truly was hopeless. All the while I was becoming increasingly depressed about the whole situation. This wasn't helped by the fact that I had a crush on a fellow student who was on the same course and lived in the same halls of residence. She was a lovely person and tried to support me as much as she could. Unfortunately for me she didn't feel the same way I did, which at the time was pretty devastating.

In 1988 there was no disabled student grant or support for students with disabilities. I basically had nowhere to turn, no equipment on which to take notes or produce essays, and had no one to read for me on to audio tape. I felt completely helpless. I needed to decide whether I was going to stay on or leave. It was also coming up to Christmas and I was really looking forward to going home, and I knew that if I stayed on for more than one term and seven weeks I would have to pay the student grant back if I dropped out. On top of these decisions I had to make, I was also losing weight. I had lost my appetite due to feeling so low. I remember feeling physically sick due to the stress and pressure I was under. My friends were really worried about me.

When I returned after Christmas I went to see the student counsellor. I poured out my heart to him. I told him how I wasn't coping on the course, how I might have to leave, and about my unrequited love. He asked me whether I needed a hug. I thought it an odd question, but answered, "Yes." He came across and put his arms around me and gave me a big hug! I was rather embarrassed. I didn't think he was talking about a big hug from him; rather, I wanted a big hug from the girl I was in love with. Oh well.

The call home was a massive relief for me. My dad was extremely understanding and drove up from London to collect me. It was around February 1989. The last couple of weeks at poly were strange. I didn't go to any lectures or tutorials and it felt very much like I was in limbo. Even though I was relieved to be going, I felt angry at the same time. Angry that I couldn't finish the course, and frustrated that my failing eyesight was responsible for creating a situation over which I had no control. Above all I felt anger again that this was happening to me. It wasn't fair. The reason I had to pull out wasn't because I was thick or unable to cope intellectually with the course, but more the fact that I had no proper support or skills to cope with my blindness. I remember that one of my friends actually remarked that she thought I hadn't come to terms with my blindness. I felt so cross with her at the time. What did she know? I thought I had come to terms with it. I was carrying a cane, I was happy to talk about my blindness, so of course I had come to terms with it. In actual fact she was quite right. I hadn't, and I had a lot to learn regarding how to cope with my blindness and how it was to shape my identity. This was going to take many years, and probably still is a work in progress.

When I got home, back down in Brixton, I had to think about my next move. What was I going to do for the rest of that year? I decided to consider the possibility of doing a couple of A Levels in one year at South London College. The course would start in September, so I had a bit of time to kill. I hung out with my old school friend Chris and we started up a new band. Chris advertised for a guitarist and singer in the music magazine *Loot*. We auditioned a guy called Andy, who was pretty good. He could sing vaguely in tune and was a pretty good guitarist. We rehearsed and played a small number of gigs. Our music could best be described as very noisy and heavy. It was great fun! In many ways I found it therapeutic.

When I started college that September it felt really strange, and almost like I was going backwards. I chose to do history and government and politics. I got in with some really cool guys on my course and started spending more time with this Caribbean guy called Paul, who had his own flat, where he often invited a few of us for parties. I thought it was amazing he had his own pad – how awesome. It was on the first floor, and as I remember he had a small kitchenette and just one room that was basically his bedroom and living room combined. For such a young guy he seemed to have his life sorted. I was really intrigued by him and wondered about his background and family, but he never discussed any of that stuff with me.

That year, 1989 to 1990, was great fun with lots of parties with my college friends, but it was also a time for me to start to focus on how I was going to go about studying and revising for my exams. I still had enough sight in one eye to be able to read using a strong light behind me. Also, I got a very small grant from the RNIB to buy a typewriter. I used to be bent over the typewriter trying to see what I had written, and inevitably ended up with terrible back pain, which was probably not helped by the fact that I had started lifting free weights. I started lifting weights after coming back from Leicester Poly, partly as a way of venting my frustration regarding dropping out and partly in an attempt to bulk up. Unfortunately I didn't know what I was doing and I just ended up injuring myself. There were occasions when I was in so much pain I couldn't walk due to severe sciatica. This problem was to dog me for the next couple of decades.

All my friends seemed to think that I found the A Levels a breeze. They used to say to me, "Yes, Haseeb, but it's really easy for you. You don't have to work that hard and you get good grades." Little did they know how much of a struggle it was to read and type up my essays. But I was determined to ensure that I got the grades I needed to get back to university.

The stress increased near exam time, as per usual. It's the sort of time when people stop talking to each other or relationships become strained. I was looking forward to getting the exams over and done with and resuming normal relations with my college buddies.

With exam time over, it was time to chill over the summer, waiting for the results to land on the hall carpet. I had applied to do sociology at a number of universities including York and Leicester. My brother had taken a shine to York, so I put down Leicester as my first choice. I really didn't want to end up in the same university as Toseef, because I thought it might be better for us to be independent of one another. I loved my brother but it was important for us to have our own friendship networks and time apart to grow as individuals. All I needed was a C and a D to get to Leicester. When the results came through I had achieved an A and a B. I was really chuffed. My father was even more delighted!

My second attempt at university was more successful than my first. However, going back to university was still a nerve-racking experience, for the first year at any rate. This time, I knew I was better prepared in general but that didn't detract from the fact that I had to make new friends, learn to cope in completely new surroundings and overcome my fears of failure. No mean feat, then! When I got to Leicester University I stayed at College Hall on Knighton Church Road. It was a 1960s-built complex, very basic but to all intents and purposes functional and pleasant. I was in Block C on the ground floor. I quickly made friends. I always made sure that I introduced myself to the guys around me, on my corridor and when I was at the bar. I became good friends with a second-year student called Dave, who was a gentle soul from a village just outside of Hull. I remember the first time we went off to the pub and I asked whether I could hold on to his elbow. He gave me a funny look and laughed nervously. I quickly realised that maybe he may think that I was trying to proposition him! When I explained that I needed to hold his elbow in order to be guided the penny dropped.

University always throws together some interesting characters and I got to know a good few. There was one particular guy I remember who used to read on tape for me. On one occasion I went off to the bathroom to have a shower. He finished off whatever he was reading for me and when I got around to listening back to the chapter on German economic history, he had decided to intersperse the text he read with swear words. Maybe he thought I didn't listen back to the stuff he read for me or maybe he did it to entertain himself, I don't know, but in any case I later discovered that he had a blow-up doll sat in one corner of his room. This guy wasn't normal by my standards!

At Leicester University I got a lot more support. I have to say that the welfare office were fabulous. Clare, who was the head of welfare at the time, helped me to apply for a disabled student grant, from which I was able to buy a PC with special software loaded on to it to magnify the words on the screen, together with a printer. This was a massive help. I also was able to pay fellow students to read on tape for me. This was a massive leap forward in comparison to my previous experience. The library was also brilliant. I used to go to the library and one of the staff would help me to find the books I wanted, and if necessary photocopy any chapters I needed. I would always make sure that as soon as I got my assignments, I would get down to the library and get right down to getting my books and any photocopies, and organise the reading of these on tape. Once things were on tape I could start listening and writing up my essays. It was a long, drawn-out process but it had to be done. My friends were brilliant and really supportive. I was fully aware that they were not only having to do their own assignments, but on top of that they were reading on to tape for me, which I appreciated immensely.

The other difference for me was the fact that the university campus was so compact. It was much easier for me to get around and navigate between buildings. If I got lost I simply asked someone and I was soon directed to the right building. These were the days before GPS of course. Although I didn't mind asking for help and being guided, I was determined to be as independent as possible. There was no way I wanted to repeat the experience of Leicester Polytechnic.

As my sight got worse and I became wholly dependent upon my other senses, particularly touch and hearing, I had to be ultra-organised in ensuring that all my personal possessions were in their rightful place in my room. I had always been relatively tidy, and maybe that was an automatic symptom of my worsening eyesight. However, this was critical now. I had to ensure that everything that could be labelled was labelled in large print or Braille. Things had to be in the right drawers for me to find them easily, and of course I couldn't afford for them to be lying around on the floor ready for me to trip over them. Occasionally I would put something down, like a mug, and absent-mindedly forget where I had put it. It would take wasted minutes trying to locate where I had left it! Time I could ill afford to lose. Every minute lost trying to find something could be spent doing something more useful. Even now, if someone moves something I have purposefully placed somewhere in my house and I can't find it I get extremely frustrated. So if you come and visit me and pick something up that belongs to me, please put it back where you found it!

At university I was quite enjoying the lectures and my tutorials. I made friends with a couple of mature students on my course, and one of them I got to know quite well. During my first year at Leicester University in 1990, at the first tutorial, the tutor asked us to introduce ourselves to the person next to us, exchange a few facts and then let the class know a few things about the person you just spoke to. Mary introduced herself to me and asked me a few questions. She wrote down the answers, and then I asked her a few questions and memorised what she told me. Mary didn't realise that I was blind as she didn't see me come into the room. When I recited from memory what Mary had told me about herself she told me later that she thought I was showing off! I think she must have been impressed though, as we then went for coffee with another friend downstairs at The Pit, which was in the basement of the Student Union building. The Pit doubled up as a gig venue in the evenings or a disco, depending upon what was going down in any particular week.

The first year was very important for me. I was very focused on getting through. However, with all the support and my newfound confidence I was doing okay. I did manage to find time to let my hair down and I recall plenty of occasions when I was at the student bar or in the pub, relaxing in the company of my new friends. By the time I got to the Christmas holidays there was no doubt that I would be going back to university in an upbeat and positive frame of mind.

On my return to university, things were looking positive as I churned out one essay after the other and got the grades I needed. However, I still needed to pass my exams at the end of the first year, and because of my previous university experience, where I was forced to pull out after the first term, I was still anxious to get through to the second year. If I could get through I knew I would be fine. It was just a question of taking the exams and waiting for the results. There was one set of papers that I took which I have to admit I wasn't quite sure I passed. Time would tell. It wasn't long after the exams that I found out.

CHAPTER 9

LOVE AND INTERRAILING

I was absolutely thrilled to pass the first year with pretty average marks. It didn't matter, as it wasn't going to count towards my final marks. Most of the students who had been in halls during the first year moved out. One friend, Damon, stayed in some adjoining accommodation, which was nice as he helped me out quite a bit during the second year. We used to go swimming every Wednesday (which I looked forward to), at St Margaret's swimming pool, which has since been knocked down.

What I remember of the second year of uni is the endless partying, trips to the bar and falling in love. A new set of students moved into my corridor and I quickly made a few friends, Rick, Mark, Richard and Mike. They were a great bunch of guys. Mark, who was doing economics, was extremely bright and was constantly coming into my room and asking me endless questions on any sociology-related essay assignments he had. He also tended to play quite a few pranks on me. We had air vents above our doors which could be knocked open, and he would knock mine open and squirt his water gun through it. I'd be getting off to sleep and suddenly feel water sprinkling on my head and face. I had to nail the flap shut in the end! Being blind made no difference to my buddies – I was just a regular guy to them and I gave as good as I got.

I felt very relaxed now, as I knew I was going to be okay

in respect of my studying and getting through the rest of the degree. It was now a question of how well I would do. However, as I had sacrificed so much in the first year in terms of getting out and socialising I was finding that in the second year I was most probably going in the other direction, but it felt good and I was definitely enjoying myself! Yet, I still felt lonely on those occasions when I was on my own in my room. I really wanted someone special in my life, with whom I could share those intimate moments. Someone I could talk to and who would really understand me.

Things got very interesting after the Easter holidays of 1992. Mary and I were in the same tutorial group, and on the same course. She helped me out considerably when I got a little stuck around assignment deadlines or with practical stuff. For example, I needed to get to a hospital appointment once and she came with me, and on another occasion I needed to get to the train station and she gave me a hand getting to the station and onto the train. We were starting to spend more and more time together.

After the Easter holiday I remember visiting Mary at the house she was sharing with another friend, Marian. When I got there Mary was in a very odd mood. Usually she was quite chatty and friendly, but now she seemed quiet and distant. She told me that she had got a cookbook over the Easter holidays and I half-jokingly suggested that she might want to cook me dinner. I didn't get a response, so I made my excuses and left to go back to my room in the halls. I had only got five minutes up the road when I heard someone running up behind me. It was Mary. She told me that she would be happy to ask me to dinner, but it would have to be the following weekend. I said that was fine, but was confused to say the least.

To be honest I wasn't sure how I felt about Mary at this point. I really liked her, but there was an age gap between us –

thirteen years to be precise. Also, we were on the same course in the same tutorial group. If we were to get together and it went wrong it could be quite awkward.

The following weekend came around very quickly. Mary made me an excellent Chinese meal including handmade spring rolls and stir-fry chicken with noodles. After dinner she came over and sat next to me, leant over and kissed me tenderly on the lips. I didn't expect that at all! From that point we officially became a couple. I became a regular visitor to 514 Welford Road and my life had just got a good injection of romance. But it was much deeper than that also. Mary was so incredibly supportive throughout my degree. She would regularly help me out with reading in the library, and we spent most of the time together going to lectures and tutorials. We were practically inseparable.

The weeks flew by and reality kicked back in. It was exam time again. The social sciences always appeared to take exams before the science students and by mid June my exams were over. I did a lot of my revision over at Mary's – well, as much as I could focus on. After the exams we spent a great deal of time together. I remember going on lots of walks, trips to the cinema and cooking meals together. It was so nice, but I had to get back to London and Mary to Birmingham. Mary had a house which she was renting to some nurse friends, so was staying with her parents over the summer. I went back down to Brixton to my family.

I caught up with my friends during the summer, hooked up with my friends from the band and rehearsed to play a gig at the Sir George Robey pub. Mary and I had made plans to go Interrailing over the summer and she came down a few days before we set off in early July. She came to watch the gig, which I think she probably just about tolerated! It was loud and heavy but incredibly enjoyable to pull off. In fact the pub management wanted us to go back and play another gig on another day. We never did go back, and in fact it was our last gig together.

Mary and I really wanted to get away for a few weeks and thought it would be really exciting to go Interrailing. I gave no thought to the practical challenges we might face as a result of my visual impairment. We popped along to the Student Union and bought our tickets, which were so cheap compared to today's prices. My ticket was only £26! We took a coach from Victoria coach station down to Dover and boarded a ferry to Calais. There was no Eurostar in those days. Our amazing adventure was about to start.

Once we got to Calais, we pretty much found the next train to Paris. So far, so good. On getting to Paris we booked into a hotel very near the Eiffel Tower called Le President. We visited all the tourist places you visit in Paris, which was great. However, it was pretty clear that I was going to be very dependent upon Mary for navigation and on a day-to-day basis. At home, once I was in familiar surroundings I could be fairly independent. It was the simple things like popping down to the shops or fixing myself a cup of tea in a kitchen where I knew where everything was. I had to rely upon Mary for almost everything and it was probably harder on her than it was for me. I remember feeling particularly guilty that I couldn't do more to help, such as read a map and work out directions. I did try to learn some very basic French from a simple phrase book we picked up somewhere, which did help a little when trying to ask directions to the bank in Paris. However, to all intents and purposes I was out of my comfort zone and wholly dependent on Mary. I have to admit I found this very difficult, and I know Mary did for different reasons. This holiday was either going to make us or break us.

Yet, I did discover that I could lend a helping hand when it came to the Paris Métro underground system. As I was so used to the London Underground I was somehow able to work out which direction we needed to go. The general principle seemed to be the same. But that's where the similarities stopped. I wasn't sure whether I liked Paris, to be honest. It wasn't so much the places of interest, but more the French people in the city. People seemed very tense, almost uptight. I felt as though I wasn't trusted somehow – it was a strange feeling. We moved to a one-star hotel in a downtown area of Paris. It was not the best place we were to stay in, but functional. After we left our belongings in the hotel room we went out for some more sightseeing and as we went down the stairs Mary noticed a couple of guys coming up to fumigate another room. I got that sinking feeling you get when you know you've made a bad decision. To top it all, I managed to step in some dog poo that day and brought it back into the room! Paris is full of dog poo. I don't think the concept of picking up after your dog has entered into Parisian culture.

From Paris we went to Chamonix. It was a long journey on the TGV. I have to say that the trains were fantastic and ran like clockwork, quite unlike the UK. I also had the ambition of going on the bullet train before the holiday was over. For now it was exciting enough travelling up to the mountains. Once we got to Chamonix we found the nearest tourist information office and booked ourselves into a B&B. The accommodation was marked on a map for us, and off we set to find it. Little did we know that this was going to be a three-hour ordeal.

Both of us carried heavy rucksacks we had borrowed off Mary's brother Tony, and one of these contained a two-man tent. We weren't travelling light! It was warm but drizzling slightly. The walk to the B&B wasn't easy. The roads were steep, after all this was up in the French Alps. After walking backwards and forwards on the same road for two hours trying to find this place, some of the hotel owners spotted us and popped out to try and help. Unfortunately their own accommodation was fully booked and none of them seemed to know the location of the B&B we were looking for. I was seriously thinking that we would have to pitch our tent in someone's field.

Eventually a lovely woman pulled up in her car and looked at the map. "I know this place. I will take you," she said. We were so happy. We climbed into her car and she took us to where we needed to go. It was getting dark at this point and must have been around 8pm.

When we did get to the B&B, to our horror the landlady said to us that she had given our room away as she thought we weren't going to turn up. But then she said, "Don't worry, I have a little outhouse you can stay in. It's clean and tidy and my daughter uses it for sleepovers." We went to this little outhouse and there was a pull-out bed and some basic furniture. It was clean and we were just happy to have a roof over our heads. We had nothing to eat that evening apart from a tin of pineapples to share! Probably the best tin of pineapples I have ever tasted.

The next stop was Les Houches the following day. It was back to the tourist information centre for booking into a youth hostel. The youth hostel we stayed in was fantastic, although it was really weird staying in a room with eight other people where the beds were practically side-to-side. One evening as I entered the dorm a young woman walked in with only a towel wrapped around her. Mary said she was a little embarrassed. I don't think she realised I couldn't see her! The youth hostel was a new environment I had to get used to and I couldn't really walk around independently. It takes a while for me to navigate around a new building and I certainly didn't want to walk into a room or area I wasn't supposed to go in.

The man who owned the youth hostel lived with his wife and teenage daughter in a nearby farmhouse. He started up the youth hostel following a farming accident when he lost all of his fingers in farm machinery. It was fascinating to learn how he managed to carry all of the plates and trays when he served up dinner with stubs of the parts of his fingers which hadn't been severed. I was really impressed with how he had adapted his work life around his disability. I felt a connection between us.

During the day there were some fantastic walks where Mary could take in the views and I could inhale the fresh mountain air, listen to the chirping of birds, the wind blowing through the trees and feel the abundant, lush vegetation which dominated the rolling hills and mountainous terrain. At the end of the day we looked forward to the amazing French cooking which was served up to us by our fingerless landlord.

Next stop was a week in a campsite in Switzerland, Lauterbrunnen. This was the first campsite I had ever experienced. It wasn't easy for me as the facilities were a five-minute walk from where our tiny tent was pitched. I had to go into the male toilet and shower area alone and do my best to find the facilities and not walk into anyone. If I was lucky then some guy would help me out, but many of those staying at the campsite didn't speak English. However, somehow I coped. Yet, I felt guilty about relying so heavily on Mary and not even being able to help her to cook our evening meals. To be honest I felt a bit useless at times. I also wondered what the other campers thought about me not helping. Did they think I was a sexist guy who expected to be waited on hand and foot?

Once Mary said jokingly as I sat in the tent waiting for my dinner, "Big Chief Sitting Bull." Although she was teasing me, it was hurtful. Back home I love to help out in the kitchen and am more than capable of cooking my own meals without any assistance. Everything is done by touch, feel and taste.

Our next destination was Italy, such a contrast to France and Switzerland. For a start when we entered Italy the Italian immigration officers boarded the train. One of the immigration officers came to our compartment, which we were sharing with four other travellers. He took my full British passport and started to question Mary and me on how long we were planning to stay in Italy and where we were going. He took my passport to a colleague and it was clear that he was questioning its validity. I was quite worried. However, the other immigration officer pretty much shooed him away and he returned with my passport.

Once in Italy we made our way to Venice, which was simply stunning with all its little canal systems and quirky streets. From Venice we went to Florence and then on to Rome. We stayed in Rome for around a week, which gave us plenty of time to get to places such as the Colosseum, the Trevi Fountain and of course the Vatican. We needed more time in any case as it was absolutely roasting. Most of the residents who weren't catering to the tourists had done the sensible thing and gone on holiday to the cooler parts of Italy or beyond, so it was fairly quiet in the middle of July.

After a week of rushing around in the heat Mary and I were ready to cool off ourselves. We decided to take an overnight train to Paris, and from there a bullet train up to Brittany. However, when we went to catch the overnight train, we had got to the station too late and the train had already left. There was a little bit of a communication problem between Mary and the man who was talking to her. I couldn't really hear what was being said as I was slightly behind where Mary was standing, and when she turned around to me to ask whether I understood what the guy was saying I wasn't able to help. Well, naturally Mary found the whole situation overwhelming. She said a few words that suggested to me that she was extremely annoyed and frustrated and she walked away from me and I didn't have a clue where she had gone. In fact she was only a few yards away and could see me at all times. I wasn't to know that and it seemed like ages but it was probably only five minutes, or even less, when she wasn't in touching distance of me. I got quite upset and worried, but in my heart of hearts I knew she wouldn't just abandon me in the middle of the train station. When she came back to me I was still upset with her and gave her the silent treatment. It didn't last long – Mary had a way of bringing me out of my silly moods!

So, the following day we set off on the last part of our journey to Brittany. I got to go on the bullet train, and the last few days were very relaxing and laid-back compared to the first three weeks.

This had to be one of the most memorable and incredible experiences of our lives. Mary had been amazing. Not only had she pretty much single-handedly worked out how to get both of us through three European countries, but she had done it with a blind man in tow. Parts of the trip were extremely stressful for her and I knew that at the end of our little adventure it would either make us or break us as a couple.

On arriving home, both of us had lost a considerable amount of weight. We both weighed around eight stone due to all the walking and dry-frying on our camp cooker. It was nice getting back home to our creature comforts.

Mary went back to Birmingham shortly after we got back and I spent most of the rest of the summer bumming around in London. It was a great summer but eventually it would be time to return to university for the hardest year, a new set of students to get to know in halls, and then some decisions to make regarding my future once I had finished university. The latter was probably the most worrying part, but I put it to the back of my mind as I did have some idea of what I wanted to do. But as I was to find out, your future isn't always in your own hands.

CHAPTER 10

MARRIAGE AND CAREER

When Mary went back to Birmingham during the summer of 1992 she worked as an agency nurse at the Children's Hospital, where she had been a full-time nurse before she started at Leicester University. I planned to go and visit her. I had met her parents before we left for Europe, which was really nice. Her mum was from Listowel, Ireland and her father was from Dublin. Mary had told me that telling her parents about me wasn't particularly easy. She was a little worried about the reaction she would get when she told them that my parents were from Pakistan, and of course that I was blind. Mary imparted the information one day to her parents on her way out of the front door and left them to think about the juicy information! I completely understood how this might seem to Mary's parents. After all, I was still a student and there was no guarantee that I would get a job once I had left university.

Well, when I did meet them they were absolutely lovely and so very hospitable. I also met Sandy, the family dog. I was a little scared of dogs to be honest, not having been brought up with them, which seems so ironic now I have owned guide dogs.

Mary and I went back to university in the autumn of 1992. I decided to stay for my final year at College Hall and made some new friends. After Christmas, however, Mary and I decided that it might be better if I moved in with her and Marian. It would mean that we could share the bills and Mary could help me out. It seemed like a perfect plan. I got permission from the warden of College Hall to move out and terminate my contract. I moved in with Mary and shared her room, and we had to sleep on the floor as she only had a single bed. Even though we are not the world's biggest people, it would have been quite uncomfortable. The only problem with me moving in, though, was that we didn't tell the landlord. This was only a problem when I decided to order a desk. When it arrived the landlord decided to visit. The delivery was in my name and naturally the landlord was suspicious. So, Mary very ably covered for me, telling him that I couldn't really have the desk delivered to the halls, so I had arranged for it to be dropped off at 514 Welford Road! Luckily for me he accepted the story. However, every time the landlord turned up for rent I had to hide upstairs in the wardrobe in case he came in.

I loved living with Mary and Marian. It was great fun and so much more relaxed for me. Mary and I were so much in love. I can't remember ever having an argument or disagreement. We got on so well. I even went along with Mary's vegetarian diet! We walked into university together, went to the same lectures and pretty much were joined at the hip. It wasn't long before we started talking about what we were going to do after university. I really wanted to go on to study a master's degree in social work, and Mary was thinking the same. Also, we were starting to think about marriage, despite the fact that we had been together for only a year; it did feel like we were soulmates. I never felt the age gap at all. In fact anyone who found out about it was shocked, as Mary had very youthful looks. My friends would tell me how good-looking she was, but for me it was her kindness and caring side which bowled me over.

I applied to do the MA in social work during 1993, and was called for interview. I was extremely nervous, and prior to this had very little interview experience. In the interview I was asked what work experience I had. I had to admit that I didn't have any. The interview didn't go at all well and I knew in my heart that I wouldn't be offered a place. A couple of months later I received a rejection letter which stated this and advised that I should get some work experience. I was very disappointed but accepted the situation and wondered how I would get relevant work experience – particularly being blind, it wasn't going to be straightforward. Mary was really upset for me, more so because she knew that having a vocational qualification would mean a much greater chance of a decent career in social work for me.

Not long after I got turned down for a place at the School of Social Work, Mary spotted a job in the paper for an advocacy organisation for people with disabilities. It was for a development worker position. I applied and to my surprise got an interview. I hadn't yet graduated or indeed taken my finals, but that didn't worry me. I went for the interview and again I performed poorly. Again, this was due to lack of interview experience as well as work experience. This time, however, I got a really nice letter from Barbara Howard, the manager, on behalf of the interview panel, asking me to consider applying for other positions which were likely to be advertised in the near future.

I graduated in July with a 2.1. I was very pleased with that. It was good to get the degree out of the way. Mary and I were making plans to get married over the summer. She had sold her house in Birmingham and we set our wedding day for the 3rd September 1993. We moved into a friend's house in Groby, Leicestershire soon after we finished university. My two little brothers, who were eight and ten years old, came to visit for a few days, which was great fun and very joyous. They really liked Mary and she was great with them. I remember playing Monopoly with Shazib and Tahseen. Shazib was incredibly competitive (very similar to me) and Tahseen (the younger of the two) was really laid-back when it came to board games. When Tahseen was winning, Shazib would get extremely upset and start to cry. Mary took them swimming one day. When they got to the pool Shazib noticed that his swimming trunks were not in the kitbag. He instantly blamed Tahseen for not packing them! Fortunately the staff at reception had a spare pair they could lend to my brother.

Towards the end of summer we were asked to leave our friend's house as she wanted to move back in. We had to find somewhere really fast. That was the first time I really feared we might end up homeless. We only had a week's notice but luckily we managed to find a lovely semi-detached in Wigston Fields, Roehampton Drive. It was very spacious and even had a pear tree in the back garden. I remember my parents and brothers coming to visit us around September and taking a couple of bags full of pears home with them!

Our wedding took place on the 3rd September 1993 at a Catholic church in Harborne, Birmingham. Mary had a beautifully fitted ivory-coloured wedding dress and the bridesmaids had stunning white and peach dresses. Yasmin (my cousin), Monica (Mary's youngest sister) and Allana (my niece) were the bridesmaids and my nephew Liam was the pageboy. We had our reception at Birmingham Botanical Gardens. It was a truly fantastic day, with the exception of the best man's speech, which was pretty rubbish! I told Damon not to mention my heavy drinking sessions, but he ignored me. Never a good idea to mention this when half your guests are Muslims! Oh well, I did try to warn him. Funnily enough I've not seen him since – I always wondered what happened to Damon, my best man.

I needed to work out what I was going to do next in terms of work or career. Someone had mentioned that there was a diploma in information technology that was available for postgraduates, but you had to be from an area which was European Social Fund approved. As my place of residence had been Brixton, which fell into the ESF eligible zones, I managed to get accepted onto the course. It paid £400 a month, which would help towards bills. Mary got onto the social work course at Leicester University but for the following year, so in the meantime she applied for a job as a residential social worker and got it. The shifts were unsociable at times, but again, it all helped.

I started my course in October and hated every minute of it. I did learn something about how to use more advanced IT applications but found the course dry and quite frankly pointless. In December Mary spotted another job with the voluntary sector organisation I had applied to earlier in the year. It was part-time, twenty hours a week and around £12,000 pro rata, which worked out at around £400 a month. A job was a job and I did not hesitate in applying.

I got called for interview, but I got cold feet. My brother Toseef was coming to visit and I was unprepared for the interview. When I look back I can't believe what I did, but I rang up to tell a white lie. I said that I couldn't come to interview on the day they were asking me to come as the roof had leaked due to the storm the previous night. It wasn't true, but got me out of a pickle. To my surprise they contacted me later that week to ask whether I would come for interview on another day. I agreed, and this time I did turn up. I made sure that I prepared well, had done my homework and even went as far as providing Braille notes for one of the interview panel members who I knew was a Braille user. When I walked out of the interview room I felt good. I knew I had done a much better job this time than previously and was keeping my fingers crossed. Later that afternoon I got the call from Barbara telling me that she was offering me the job. I was so happy. Yes! My first job, and a chance to prove myself.

I didn't hesitate in handing in my notice to Leicester University. They were very pleased for me; as far as they were concerned the ESF-funded course was geared towards getting people into employment. Win-win. I started my job as an advocacy worker in January 1994 and worked for FAIRDEAL for two and a half years. I learned a lot and the manager, my fellow colleagues and the management committee were incredibly supportive.

After around six months the job turned into a full-time role, although I had to apply for the other seventeen hours through an open recruitment process. The organisation, quite rightly, took their equality of opportunity very seriously. During my time at FAIRDEAL I supported people with disabilities through community care assessments, complaints and accessing public health services. It was a real privilege working with Barbara, who really knew her stuff around advocacy and helping disabled people, particularly those who were very vulnerable, such people with learning disabilities, have a voice and a say in their own lives. Barbara was a qualified social worker by profession. She didn't have to work in the voluntary sector but she chose to because the values at FAIRDEAL fitted with her beliefs. She was incredibly supportive of me and I always got the impression that she wanted to give me enough support and encouragement to help me develop, but not too much, in order to keep my feet on the ground.

However, it wasn't all plain sailing. I needed to get support from Access to Work, which is a government-run scheme which assists disabled people in employment. The centrally-funded scheme allows disabled people to buy specialist equipment and employ support workers. I needed both of these, and was entitled to support. It took around nine months for the help to come through. I had my own computer from university at this time, which really helped, but no one to help me to get out and about to home visits. I had to manage on public transport using my white cane to get around. It wasn't exactly easy. Eventually the help came after a lot of toing and froing with the Job Centre, who managed the approval process. This didn't go without incident. Two disability employment advisors came to visit my manager, and on leaving one of them called Barbara "a bitch". I was both horrified and embarrassed, and it was so far from the truth.

This job really allowed me to get to know Leicestershire quite well. I used to visit people all over Leicester and Leicestershire. Some of the people I supported were really interesting and came from all sorts of backgrounds and communities – some were very privileged and articulate, some very poor and some lacked any communication skills altogether. I worked with lots of people with disabilities, which ranged from physical to sensory and those with learning disabilities.

On one home visit to an elderly white gentleman in his seventies, after I had been conversing with him for thirty minutes or so he said, "Your English is very good, where did you learn it?"

To which I replied, "At school."

On another visit to a care home for people with learning disabilities the manager of the home struck up a conversation with me and asked when I had left school – was it last year? I was twenty-four years old, wore glasses and I guess I must have looked very young. I don't think I look so fresh these days!

Working for this charity organisation gave me so much confidence and lifted my self-esteem to new heights. My colleagues respected me and I really felt valued for my contribution to the organisation, and I was actually helping other disabled people. I was really happy at FAIRDEAL.

I got the opportunity to work with student social workers while working there, which proved to be mutually beneficial. I would often be shadowed by them on home visits to service users. On one such occasion a student social worker accompanied me on a home visit to a gentleman who was very well known to social services. He was well known, so I'd heard, because of his violent outbursts. I heard that he had attacked his elderly mother, but his story was that he was having an epileptic fit at the time. Anyway, we visited this guy, who lived in a very poor part of Leicester in his council house. When we got to the house there was a great big sign that said, *Beware of dangerous dog*.

The student social worker, who wasn't keen on dogs, tucked in behind me and said, "Haseeb, you don't mind if you go in first? I'm scared of dogs." I thought, *You're not going to last long as a social worker, mate*. I actually bumped into this guy a few years ago and I was right: he no longer practises social work!

While working for FAIRDEAL I was really interested to continue with my education. I saw a part-time Master's course being run at Loughborough University in policy, organisation and changes in professional care. I think the cost was £600 a year with a day release for attending lectures. I approached Barbara to see whether they would support me to do the course, and to my absolute delight the management committee agreed. It was amazing, really. Firstly, how many courses these days cost £600 a year to do? Secondly, there aren't many voluntary sector organisations who would support their staff to do a postgraduate course and allow them to take one day a week, paid, to do it.

When I started the course I was the youngest on it. All of the other professionals doing the course were at least ten years older and so I probably had the least experience. Nonetheless, it was really interesting. It was this course and working for FAIRDEAL which first got me thinking seriously about taking up equality and diversity work as a possible future career. It was just a question of the right opportunity popping along. I was full of hope and optimism.

CHAPTER 11

FAMILY, PROMOTION AND APPLYING FOR MY FIRST GUIDE DOG

While at FAIRDEAL around 1995 I applied for a job at Leicester City Council. It was a six-month temporary contract working in equalities. I took the tough decision not to go for interview as I had a permanent job and didn't want to take any risks in case the council job wasn't extended.

In September 1995 Mary and I went for a two-week holiday to Pakistan. My parents and my brothers were all living in the same house in Lahore. It was a real culture shock for Mary, and even myself as I only had childhood memories of the country.

We spent the first week in Lahore being visited by relatives on my father's side and my mum's sisters and dad. The first thing my grandfather asked me was how much I earned. I wasn't quite sure how to answer this question as it's not something you get asked in England, straight out like that. I tried to evade the question at first but I could see that my grandfather was getting rather annoyed, so I relented and told him.

Mary and I got very ill within twenty-four hours of arriving in Pakistan. I think it's pretty much unavoidable. We drank water which had been boiled, but somehow our immune systems couldn't ward off nasty bugs. We lost a lot of weight during our stay over the two weeks.

My father decided that he wanted to give us all a tour of Pakistan, so arranged for a tour guide to take us by minibus up to North Pakistan to the Himalayas. We went through Islamabad, Rawalpindi and Tesla, and stayed in a very famous holiday destination of Murree. My grandparents also came along, although my grandmother was finding the journey very challenging. She wasn't in good health anyway and the roads weren't exactly great. Once we had got to the mountains we had to transfer to jeeps. Some of the mountain roads were windy and treacherous in places. We also had to go through Kashmir, which was heavily militarised. It was very handy that our tour guide happened to be an ex-police officer, and he handled all the border control issues. All in all, the trip was unbelievable on several levels. One thing is for sure: there is no way at this moment in time, given the political situation in Pakistan and the surrounding area, that anyone from the West could go and visit that region without jeopardising their safety. For me what stood out in going to the Himalayas was how they contrasted with the Alps. The region seemed so much more rugged, and of course it was incredibly underdeveloped where there was civilisation. But it had its own beauty and allure. Although I couldn't see it, I definitely felt its awe and glory.

In the city I remember the abject poverty that most people lived in. This was a stark contrast to the middle and upper classes, who built big houses with walls around them to create their little havens. The only time they were exposed to the poverty around them was if they needed to make a trip to a friend or to another neighbourhood for shopping etc.

Mary once said to me when we were out for a trip in the car, "Haseeb, if you could only see how poor this place is."

My little brother, who was around nine years old at the time, said, "Haseeb doesn't need to see how poor it is, he can smell it." It was true, as the smell of sewage was everywhere.

Mary started her social work course in October 1995. She managed to do her first placement at FAIRDEAL and she was in the same office as me. We didn't really work together but it was lovely to be able to go swimming before work and catch up at lunchtime. There was a great little café in the building, which sold delicious cobs and wonderful doughnuts. Those doughnuts were divine; crispy on the outside with a light dusting of sugar and a sumptuous strawberry jam filling. Mouth watering indeed!

Mary and I had been planning to try for a baby for a few months and it seemed to make sense to time any pregnancy for when Mary finished her course. So, we started trying over the Christmas holiday. In January Mary took a pregnancy test and it was positive! Just to make sure, she took a couple more. Yes, they were positive too. We were over the moon. Everything seemed to be going well. However, at around twenty weeks Mary had a heavy bleed. We went straight down to A&E and a doctor examined Mary. Thankfully everything was fine and we were naturally very relieved and the pregnancy went on as normal.

In April 1996 Mary spotted an equalities job going at Charnwood Borough Council. The starting salary was around £17,000. I applied and got an interview. I had to do quite a bit of homework in order to prepare for the job, and get hold of some national guidance in order to prepare for the presentation. There was no internet at that time, so I had to go out of my way and make an appointment with the local Race Equality Council and buy a copy of the guidance. I really wanted this job and knew I couldn't take any short cuts in my preparation for the interview. I went to town with the presentation and felt very confident going into the interview. It went very well indeed and I was offered the job. I was thrilled at the prospect of starting my first local authority job. Things were going well.

However, working for the public sector was going to be a real contrast from my experience in the charity sector. The main difference I felt was the formality and bureaucracy I encountered. Things took an incredibly long time to do. Reports would have to be written for every decision and these often bounced backwards and forwards from various senior managers and committees.

On my first week at CBC I met the chief executive. I wasn't quite sure how to address him so I asked, being the polite young man I was. His answer was, "When I was a clerk starting out in my first job, I used to address my manager as 'sir', but you can call me Mr Peatfield." And so I did. Fortunately for me my actual manager and I were on first-name terms. However, Mr Peatfield was a colourful character and told me at every opportunity about his disabled son who had abnormal feet. He once took me out in his sports car to a radio interview. At every traffic light we came to he would cut his engine to save the environment and fuel consumption. I thought it rather odd. Surely if he wanted to save the environment he might want to buy a smaller car? I don't think his ego would have allowed it.

I remember writing my first report for my manager and getting it red-penned. I felt a bit put out as every page had a correction on it or a comment of some kind. However, later I was to reflect that Steve, who had considerable experience in local government, helped me to develop and hone my report-writing skills. He was a fantastic manager and a decent guy. The most important thing was that he believed in me. That meant a lot.

At any rate, I was constantly worried about performing as well as someone who could see. I really felt that I had to perform not only as well as, but better than my able-bodied colleagues. I took every opportunity to do everything thrown my way. But the job was tough, particularly when delivering equality training. I had to pretty much memorise everything. Although I had a computer which had a speech function on it, it wasn't a laptop PC. Besides which, I couldn't really listen to notes and deliver training at the same time. It's a good job my memory is rock solid. I recall training the finance department, who were particularly challenging. They didn't want to attend the mandatory equalities training. I felt their anger at me during the interactive part of the workshop. I certainly didn't enjoy that part of my job, but it taught me to be more resilient and able to handle those sorts of scenarios without taking things personally. Yet, on the other hand I know I had many colleagues who were fascinated by how I was able to function normally. I would often get asked the question as to how I wrote reports and managed to get around the building. These were days before I got a Guide Dog. People also marvelled at my ability to memorise large amounts of information. Although I must have made it look easy, it wasn't and still isn't. Although, I do think it's easier now than it was when I first set out in my career as I've fine-tuned many of the skills I was still learning back then.

Whilst at Charnwood BC the most wonderful thing in my life happened. On the 2nd October 1996, at 8.06pm my beautiful, gorgeous daughter was born. She was born via C-section as Mary had been in labour for over twenty hours and poor Ayeisha was becoming distressed.

The anaesthetist, Mark, was brilliant, constantly telling me what was happening and reassuring me throughout the procedure. "Don't worry, Mr Ahmad, the doctor is very experienced. She'll do a very neat stitch and you won't even know that your wife had surgery."

In any event, when Ayeisha had been weighed and her fingers counted she was wrapped in a blanket and put straight into my arms. Oh, what a wonderful feeling of joy and love that overcame me. Tears welled in my eyes. It was the happiest day of my life. Ayeisha felt so small and vulnerable in my arms. I touched her tiny soft face, and she felt beautiful to me. Both Mary and

Ayeisha stayed in hospital for a few days while Mary recovered from the op. When she and Ayeisha came home Mary wasn't allowed to lift or drive so I carried out all the domestic tasks as best I could. Mary had cooked meals which we had pre-frozen which helped immensely. Our next door neighbours, Fred and Thelma, were also brilliant and took me to the supermarket for the weekly shop. These were happy days.

Everyone at work was so lovely and kind in their congratulations, and bought Ayeisha a little present. It was a soft toy with a dog head and a ring shape for the body. She loved it.

Overall, I thoroughly enjoyed my five years at Charnwood BC. I worked with some fantastic people including Anthony Gimpel, who was my support worker for a great part of my time at the council. Anthony was the son of Jewish immigrants from post-war Germany. He was in his fifties and had moved to Loughborough a few years previously. He was a well-educated man but wasn't in full-time employment when he answered a request for volunteer readers I had made to the local voluntary bureau. When I said to Anthony that I could pay him to support me he was delighted. Anthony turned out to be such a wonderful, kind and gentle soul from whom I learned so much. He helped me to organise and commemorate the very first Holocaust Memorial Day in January 1997, one of the most moving and deeply touching events I have been involved in. I remember persuading Redland Quarry to donate and organise the delivery of a large memorial stone to be installed in Queen's Park, Loughborough.

While at Charnwood BC I made sure that I took regular trips to the swimming pool, which was only a ten-minute walk away, perfect for that afternoon swim. I used to pop down a couple of times a week and it was a great stress-buster, breaking up the day nicely. I wasn't a particularly great swimmer (in fact I was extremely bad), but I could certainly go up and down the lanes.

In those days, I used to swim with fellow swimmers in the same lane, trying very carefully not to swim into them. One day I got chatting to an Italian guy who happened to be a baker. He told me he was in his sixties, and when he told me that he knocked out sixty lengths of the twenty-five-metre pool in twenty minutes, I was astounded. As we chatted in the changing room I could tell, just based on where his voice was being projected from, that he was shorter in height than me, and I'm not that tall! Anyway, he, bless his cotton socks, decided to try and teach me to swim. In his heavily accented Italian voice he would demonstrate how I should be swimming with very elaborate hand movements.

"You should put your arms in this position and try to breathe both sides." I was really chuffed that he was trying to teach me but I just couldn't comprehend his visual demonstration. In the end he said, "Oh, don't worry" and gave up his little swimming lessons.

He wasn't the only person who tried to teach me to swim a correct stroke. Years later when I was swimming in Nottingham I was approached by another fellow swimmer who offered to coach me. I didn't take up his offer either. I just didn't feel the need to improve my stroke, and secondly, I wasn't convinced that a sighted person could teach me how to swim. I was wrong of course, as I was to find out a few years later.

In 2001 I applied to Leicester City Council for a generic policy officer role. I had been at Charnwood BC for five years and I didn't want to commute any more. I was getting fed up with the moody taxi drivers at Loughborough train station and so was walking to the council offices – not so easy when you are using the white cane. The Leicester City Council interview process involved an assessment centre and an interview. I hadn't experienced a two-stage interview before so was naturally a little nervous. The strangest part was the group assessment. This is where you are thrown in with other candidates and given a scenario to discuss. There were around four other candidates I remember, and one guy instantly picked up the flipchart pen and started to facilitate the session. *Oh yes*, I thought, *he is very confident and I bet he knows he is going to get the job.* When it came to the interview I felt I did really well and had that gut feeling that I may just have done myself proud.

There were four jobs going altogether. I was offered the two-year temporary contract. Mr Confident did get the most prestigious job supporting the leader of the council. My job eventually became permanent and I got some incredible experience across a range of policy work. I was at Leicester City Council from 2001 to 2004. Towards the end of my time during 2004 I applied for a temporary secondment to develop the council's public sector agreement with central government. It was a big step up from what I was doing and I didn't rate my chances against people who had much more experience of policy than me. However, I took a very positive approach to the interview process. What did I have to lose? So, I decided to prep for the interview and just enjoy myself. I memorised pretty much all the background reading I needed to, which boosted my confidence going into the interview. After all, I wasn't going to get the job, was I?

Coming out of the interview I knew I had done well. However, to my shock and utter surprise, I got the job offer. I think I really did put a few noses out of joint among my colleagues, but I couldn't help the fact that I gave better answers than they did. Yes, the young blind guy nailed the job! It was truly unbelievable to me.

At the time I had also put in a job application for a senior equality officer post at Leicestershire County Council. Well, I accepted the temporary secondment PSA officer job and started in earnest, organising meetings to try and get colleagues interested in putting forward ideas to develop stretch targets in areas such as housing and education. It was well out of my comfort zone and to be honest, for the first time I really didn't think I could pull it off.

I got called to interview for the equality officer post at Leicestershire County Council. It was a senior position, paid the same as the secondment job I had taken on and it was permanent. I did well at interview and got a job offer. I was in a bit of a dilemma. Should I stay and complete the secondment and move away from equality and diversity work, or should I take on the job at the county council, which was much more within my comfort zone and what I enjoy doing? To be frank there was no competition – the equality officer job won out. There were too many politics at play at the city council for my liking, particularly the office politics. The move to the county council was in the end a good one for me as it took me on to bigger and better things.

I really enjoyed my role at the county council and certainly learned a lot from my manager, Barry Davies. Barry had worked for many years in social services and rose through the ranks and was now the assistant director of partnerships and diversity. He was responsible for over four hundred staff and was now on a very good salary managing a handful of employees.

"It's the best job I've ever had," he once told me. Barry was and is an extremely knowledgeable man from very humble beginnings. His father died when he was very young, in his early teens, and he and his brother had to help his mum on their farm in Wales. This, I think, gave Barry a very pragmatic and no-nonsense approach to life and his work. Barry was tough but fair. I had a couple of disagreements with him but actually I really respected the man and still do. He retired around 2009 but we still meet up and go for occasional drinks with other ex-Leicestershire County Council friends.

In 2007 I applied for my first head of service job at

Nottingham City Council. This was a massive step up for me, and again I didn't expect to get it. But get it I did! I was over the moon. The head of equality and diversity job was every little bit as tough as its title suggests. I was at Nottingham City Council for six years. I had a brilliant team around me whom I carefully recruited including Shakeel Khalil (team leader, confidant and right-hand man), Nicky Gibson and Vincent Bryce. I also had a wonderful support worker, Emily Jones, a lovely, sweet and light-hearted soul.

Life was good for a while at work. However, the ravages of cutbacks and people moving on meant that the last couple of years at Nottingham (2011–2013) became extremely challenging. The commute backwards and forwards and trying to fit in training and family life took their toll on me. Mary spotted a job in Leicester with slightly less pay and responsibility and I jumped at the chance of getting a job closer to home. I rocked up to the interview and nailed it. On reflection it was definitely the right move. Less commuting meant more time with the family and of course, training. It made a world of difference in terms of my energy levels as I was less fatigued physically and mentally. Instead of getting home at 7pm from Nottingham and then hitting the gym, I can now leave work at 4pm and be done and dusted by 6pm. It's so fantastic! Furthermore, I have a wonderful team I work with including a brilliant support worker, Abby Eames, who I get on with so well. It makes the world of difference when you have someone who works with you who you trust, and who loves your dog! I have to say I have never met anyone as kind and caring and generous as Abby. She is an exceptional human being.

It was about the time when I was due to go for my current job at Leicester City Clinical Commissioning Group in January 2013 that my first guide dog Quin suddenly died. It was a shock. The decision to apply for my first guide dog was the result of an accident I had going home from work one day. I was a year into my job at Leicestershire County Council, when during November 2004 I was walking home from work. I had just got off the bus and was using my white cane as usual to help me get up the road. I had a habit of walking very fast, swinging my cane in front of me. The worst that had happened to me previously was that I might accidently scrape my knuckle on a lamp post, or worse, actually walk into it as a result of going too fast. On this occasion, I had just started walking up Rosemead Drive, which was literally five minutes from my house, and my cane swung under a skip parked in front of someone's front garden. My midriff went straight into the side of the skip and I doubled over with pain. In fact, I ended up on the ground as the pain was so bad. A couple walking towards me asked me if I was okay, and because of the embarrassment I said I was fine, straightened up and carried on walking the best I could. I never actually went to A&E but I now realise, having read a considerable amount regarding the symptoms surrounding fractures, that I had most probably cracked a rib or two. I couldn't swim for a few weeks and it took me a good six months to heal properly from my injury.

This incident made me think very seriously about the dangers I often exposed myself to in trying to get around on a daily basis. I thought that I had got off quite lightly on this occasion. What would happen if next time I hit my head against an object jutting out when walking along a street? I quickly came to the conclusion that it was time to apply for a guide dog. I had been toying with the idea for a while but this incident accelerated my decision. It was simply getting too dangerous for me to be trying to get around using a white cane. I was already having to catch two buses to get to County Hall for work and it was very tiring mentally and physically. So, I rang up the Guide Dogs for the Blind Association, made some enquiries, got sent some forms, filled them in and applied for my first guide dog. I was told that it would take up to two years before I might get a dog, however, I should be on standby in any case as one may become available at short notice.

In the meantime, I got the opportunity to 'test-drive' a dog, who was brought to me at County Hall. It was a completely different experience to walking with a white cane. When using a cane, you are very much in contact with the world around you. What I mean is that the cane is in your hand and you are dragging it along the floor and any time it hits an object you know there is something there. Whereas with a guide dog it pretty much walks you around any object and there is no contact with the immediate environment other than your feet on the ground. The dog stops when you get to a curb edge and you have to tell it to go forward, or to the left or right. Although you are in control, you are also not in control as the dog guides you to where you want to go. To be honest I loved the smooth feeling of being guided by a dog but still didn't really appreciate how much it would change my life.

I soon got the call to attend guide dog training in Leamington Spa. Work were great and allowed me to take two weeks off to train with Quin. So, it was off to guide dog school for me!

CHAPTER 12

THE MIGHTY QUIN, MY FIRST GUIDE DOG

I went to guide dog training in June 2005 and was partnered with a gorgeous pale yellow Labrador called Quin. I had met him a couple of months previously for a brief introduction and "test drive". However, I was going to spend the next two weeks with Quin, getting to know him, and, of course, for him to get to know me.

Training took place in a hotel and Quin was left with me on my first day. His initial reaction was to run back to the hotel room door through which Dave, my guide dog instructor, had just exited. Quin started to cry and I thought, *Oh no, what am I supposed to do now?* Not having owned a dog before I had absolutely no idea. I sat on the floor and waited for the big guy to saunter over when he was ready. Soon enough he came across and started to sniff me. I was a bit nervous but really excited at the prospect of getting to know him.

I really didn't know what I was doing and so the training was very necessary. However, the other three people on the course were experienced owners of guide dogs and they were not impressed that they had to attend a two-week residential course. Neither were they impressed that it was taking place at a hotel. They had previously trained at the Guide Dog Centre in Leamington Spa. All these folks did for two weeks was whinge whilst I was having a blast getting to know my new best friend.

On my first outing with Quin, Dave handed me the harness and I honestly didn't know what the heck I was doing. I tried to put the harness on Quin back to front.

Dave looked at me and said, "Haseeb, what on earth are you doing?"

I replied, "Dave, I think I need a bit of help. I've never put one of these on before."

Neither had I picked up poo. This was a big topic of conversation and debate among those being trained. I was taken through a blow-by-blow account of how to go about picking up dog poo. We were told that we would be given a metal pen that would be built for us which could stand outside in our back garden for the Guide Dog to "spend" in. It was drilled into us to ensure that the dog poos in the pen before it leaves the house. Whilst guide dog owners are exempt from being fined, the Guide Dog Association are keen that we take responsibility for clearing up after our dogs wherever possible.

Finally I qualified and the real fun began. Quin and I had to learn all the routes to work and the regular places I visited such as the supermarket and swimming pool. I had to take two buses to work. Things were going really well until one day walking into work the automatic doors weren't working properly. Somehow on the way out I hit my head against the edge of one of these doors and cut my head open. Quin was so upset that the following day when we were going into work he refused to go through the doors. I knew then that he was going to be a brilliant dog.

Quin just totally changed my life. I was able to get from A to B relatively quickly and easily. A guide dog needs to be trained to know where he/she is going, so I worked quite a lot of routes with him with the help of the Guide Dog Instructor. His pace was good too – very fast, which suited me just fine. I was told a few years later that in fact Dave ended up with shin splints because he struggled to keep up with us.

Of course it's not all plain sailing or perfect. It takes a good year for someone to bond with their guide dog. I have many fond memories of Quin and his antics – being a Labrador, his eyes were always bigger than his belly. When I first brought him home I accidently left a tub of Flora Light out on the work surface one evening. I came down for breakfast and heard some crunching coming from Quin's bed. He had just polished off 500g of margarine! *Right*, I thought, *I'll remember to put that away next time.* However, a couple of days later I did the same and Quin repeated his mischief! Surprisingly, he wasn't sick.

Yes, I recall Quin was very naughty at times. He stole one of the gym staff's sandwiches and he regularly scavenged and was frequently sick as a result. However, despite being a cheeky sandwich thief, he was a real character and beautiful with it. He always had admirers wherever we went.

The question that people often ask me is how do they know where they are going? They do work regular routes but I have to tell my guide dog to turn right or left. Also, they only have the intelligence of a six-year-old so crossing roads has to be done with care. If I can find someone to cross the road with I will ask. Otherwise it can be a bit dicey.

I do have to concentrate on where I am going with my guide dogs. I remember a number of occasions when I switched off and Quin decided to head towards the park instead of home. I was completely disorientated and had to ask for help. Once I had to stop and ask a complete stranger where I was and he kindly gave me a lift home.

I had Quin for seven years. He travelled with me on all manner of public transport to Nottingham City Council. I don't think I could have done that journey easily without him. He was very popular around the office. Well, most of the time, except for one day, when he got diarrhoea in the office. He tried to run out of the building but just couldn't get out quick enough. One of the secretaries was kind enough to clean up the mess. It was pretty grim to be honest.

Sadly Quin passed away at the beginning of 2013. One day I was getting ready to go to work as normal and I got his food ready as per usual. I put it in front of him and he wasn't interested. I knew something was wrong then. He had also wet the floor, which was not like him. He was just so lethargic, so I called my good friend Chris Sherwood, who is a vet. Chris kindly popped around and checked him over. He checked his belly and teeth. He told me that the good news was that he couldn't feel any lumps but his gums were yellow so he was clearly anaemic. Mary and I took him straight to the vet and I spent the day wondering what was wrong with him. That afternoon I got a call and the vet told me that she was sorry, but that on opening Quin up, his insides were a complete mess. He had bled to death.

I just couldn't take this in. "What? He's died?"

"Yes, so sorry but he had tumours of the spleen and liver."

I was inconsolable. It was so strange not having Quin any more. I was so used to him being there in the morning when I came down to breakfast. So used to him following me around when he wanted attention. And, all of a sudden, just in the course of a few hours he had been taken away from me.

He was such a great dog. I made many friends through Quin on the train and on my travels. The most funny of these involved a guy who used to travel to and from Nottingham. I got on the train one day and was walking up the aisle and this man called over to me and asked me to sit near him.

"Sit here, mate. I love dogs... I have a hamster and my

hamster would absolutely love your dog."

I went to sit down and then the man started complaining that Quin was taking up too much space. So I thought, *I don't want to be sitting next to this strange chap*. I got back up and said I was going to the loo. I went to the next carriage and sat somewhere else. However, on getting off the train at Leicester, this guy sees me and starts to get rather animated.

He says, "I was so worried about you. I thought something had happened. I have autism so I get really worried about stuff." I felt really bad then!

I bumped into Simon quite a bit after that. He always told me about his hamster and how much he wanted his hamster to meet Quin. I also got invited to his flat on numerous occasions, which I politely declined.

On one journey while waiting for a tram some guy was standing on the opposite platform. "Hey you," he calls to me.

I looked over in the general direction of this guy.

"Yes, you with the guide dog. Is that a guide dog?"

I said, "Yes", thinking that he was going to give me some useful piece of advice.

Instead he said, "Well, you can get rid of your guide dog. Let the Lord guide you from now on."

On another journey, a woman insisted on helping Quin and me out of the train station. Despite the fact she wasn't waiting for a bus she insisted on waiting until my bus arrived. I took out my phone to text Mary to let her know I was on the way home.

This woman said, "Oh, let me text for you, I know how to text. Please let me send the text to your wife." Needless to say, I didn't hand over the phone!

After Quin died it took me nine months to get my next guide dog. Fortunately I had started a new job in early 2013 in Leicester, which made the commute much better for me. The journey to Nottingham had been taking around two and a half hours a day. I had started training for triathlons in 2008 so it was getting tough trying to balance work, family and training. It was a good move despite a slight pay cut.

I trained with Walt, a German Shepherd cross Retriever, in August 2013. He was very different to Quin – much calmer, and certainly not a scavenger. However, we still had a few teething problems.

When I first got Walt, I took him up the road to the butcher's and on the way back I could hear that the traffic seemed really close. I got to the turning off the old London Road, taking me up to Rosemead Drive.

As I walked up the road some guy pulled up in his car. He wound down his side window and asked me if I was okay.

Perplexed, I said, "Yes, why?"

"Well," he replied, "back there you were walking in the middle of the road. It looked pretty dangerous."

Indeed, Walt loves the trip to Ragg's the butcher's and never fails to stop dead outside the door. It might have something to do with the fact that the butcher's wife was sneaking him sausages for two years before I caught on to what she was doing!

CHAPTER 13

INTRODUCTION TO TRIATHLON

I can honestly say that I didn't make a conscious decision to do triathlons. It was more a case of stumbling into it by accident. I kept reasonably fit by doing some moderate exercise over the years. As a kid I was pretty active until my condition became harder to manage. Up until then I was playing football, riding a bike and dabbled in some martial arts. I was a pretty fit teenager, to all intents and purposes.

Once I became blind it became a priority for me to concentrate on my education. I had no idea that para sports were an option; however I did go to a blind sports and athletics meet in Manchester in 1989 when I was around nineteen years old. I did a couple of weeks' training and entered the one hundred metres and two hundred metres. I didn't do that well in the one hundred metres but was doing quite well in the two hundred metres until I tripped. A couple of guys told me that they thought I was really good, but then I went back down to London and there was no follow-up. I didn't think anything of this as this was around the time that I was looking to go back to university to finish off my degree after the bad experience of dropping out of Leicester Poly the previous year.

And that is pretty much what I did in 1990. I had a friend who took me swimming on a weekly basis when at university. To keep fit I also walked the mile to and from Leicester University with the assistance of my white cane (sometimes twice a day). When I got my first job I made sure I got down to St Margaret's swimming baths at least three times a week to keep fit. I could just about make out someone in front of me to follow up and down the lanes.

I remember on one occasion going to the swimming pool at lunchtime. This old fellow offered to help me out to the poolside. I was happy for him to assist. While we walked he said that it might help if I had a band around my arm telling people I couldn't see. He was a really nice, helpful old guy.

Once we got to the poolside one of the lifeguards said to this chap, "Excuse me, sir, you haven't got your trunks on." This lovely old guy was starkers!

Around the same time that I got Quin, I also started riding a tandem with a friend of mine, Richard Spicer. He did the occasional bike ride around Rutland Water, a local reservoir in Leicestershire, so he and I hired a tandem one day and rode all the way around, which is around twenty-three miles. Excited for the chance to get out and about, we then borrowed a tandem off one of his friends, but as it happened his friend asked for the tandem back so we bought a second-hand Dawes MTB tandem and started doing weekly rides. The very first time I rode with Richard Spicer, I remember buying loads of padding just in case we crashed. Fortunately nothing of the sort happened and I soon ditched the ridiculous Michelin Man-style outfit.

Around 2008 I said to Richard that I wouldn't mind trying to see if I could give running a go. The idea occurred to me as a consequence of jogging next to my guide dog. Quin loved bolting out of the house and sprinting up the road. I was told categorically not to run with the guide dog because of the inherent risk of not being able to stop quickly enough to avoid bumping into obstacles. However, I trusted Quin implicitly. But

Richard had a dodgy knee and said that he couldn't run with me but knew someone through church who might take me for a run.

So he put me in touch with another Richard. This was Richard Chipps, who was then the chairman of Leicester Triathlon Club. Richard was to become my swim coach and mentor over the next few years and he had a big hand in shaping my early years as a triathlete.

Richard Chipps and I went for a run early in 2008. It was a cold spring afternoon and we ran up the A6 along the wide path which narrowed in places, particularly where people had parked their cars on the pavement. Richard and I jogged along at a gentle pace and as we got into the run, perhaps fifteen minutes in, he asked me whether it was okay for me. I said that it was fine and that I could even speed up. I realised with great pleasure that I could go quicker but he quickly replied that he couldn't go any faster and it was clear that I was going to have to get someone speedier than me, or at least someone able to keep the same pace to run with.

I had no idea how fast I could run. I was thirty-eight years old at this time and it was anyone's guess as to what potential lay within. The fact was, I loved it. I felt free, and loved the fact that I was running on open road, which I never thought I would be able to do; it hadn't even occurred to me. Even then at that early stage I was thinking of racing and pushing my boundaries and testing my abilities against others. I spoke to Richard on numerous occasions at church and we started discussing the possibility of me doing some triathlon specifically aimed at disabled athletes. However, before I could start to even contemplate doing competitive races I had to get into open water for some swim practice.

My very first open-water swim was in May 2008. Richard said that I could probably borrow someone's wetsuit for the swim but I decided to pop along to a surf shop in Nottingham (where I was now working as the head of equality and diversity at Nottingham City Council), and bought myself an ill-fitting wetsuit. I remember the support worker at the time, who was female, told the shop assistant that if I got stuck in it when in the changing room she hoped that she wouldn't be expected to pull me out of it!

Ill-fitting wetsuit or not, I was ready for my first open-water swim. How would I get on? How cold was it going to be, and would I love it or would it be a complete disaster?

CHAPTER 14

PARATRIATHLON: THE EARLY YEARS

2008 was a really exciting point in my life. I had already started a new job in Nottingham as head of equality and diversity in 2007, and began an MA in human resource management in 2008. It was going to be a busy couple of years and the commute to and from Nottingham was challenging in itself, two and a half hours of dead time where I couldn't do any triathlon training.

Richard Chipps, chairman of Leicester Triathlon Club and lecturer at De Montfort University, was going to be a massive influence on me in my first few years as I developed into a fully-fledged triathlete. The support he gave me was phenomenal and for that I am forever in his debt. From 2008 until 2014 he gave me a tremendous amount of his personal time, providing me with three coached swim sessions a week including one on a Thursday night, which was club night so I also got to meet other people who were in the same boat and trying to get fitter and faster.

Richard was so patient and incredibly positive. He was also very innovative in his approach, trying different methods of getting me to 'feel' the water. Swimming is mostly about technique, but trying to teach someone who cannot see to swim is a massive challenge. How do you teach someone body position, for instance? Teaching swimming is a visual process requiring the teacher to demonstrate hand and body positions to the learner. If you are lucky you can look at some swim analysis done through filming the swimmer underwater. For a blind swimmer, and specifically for someone who hasn't swum properly before, you have to physically take that person through the different phases of the swim. So Richard did just that for me. Every session was tough and very frustrating for me but I kept going. I was told that eventually it would all click into place. There is no doubt that my swimming has progressively improved over the past eight years with Richard's coaching for the first four of those, and then just sheer bloody-mindedness on my part.

Swimming in a pool, even if I have my own lane, can be tricky. I recall that in the 2012 season I was training with the Leicester Triathlon Club one evening. I was swimming front crawl, got to the end and completed a touch-turn. Unfortunately I swam under the rope into another lane and had a headlong collision with another triathlete. His forehead was impaled on my ring finger, and it was the end of his session as he climbed out of the pool with a massive dent in his head. I, on the other hand, ended up with a broken finger!

Richard Chipps took me for my very first open-water swim at Watermead Country Park during May 2008. I went in wearing my surfer's wetsuit, which was way too big. The horribly cold water poured in and took my breath away. The cold penetrated my skin and got to my bones. My head felt like it had just been stuck in a bucket of ice cubes. Richard and I were tethered calf-to-calf, and as I tried to tread water I started to spin around in circles.

Richard shouted to me, "Haseeb, stop going around in circles!" But I just couldn't help myself. The cold was affecting the fluid in my inner ear, and not being able to see, I was completely disoriented. In the end Richard asked me to lie on my back and he pulled me to shore. He asked me whether I wanted to get dressed and go home. I immediately responded by saying that I wanted to get back in and have another go. I did get back in and the same thing happened again. Not perturbed, I returned the following week, and the week after that to overcome my fear of the cold water and conquer the challenge of open-water swimming. I am not one to give up easily.

Richard became a very important part of my triathlon life and assumed the role of a coach and friend. He sent me a structured training programme with different zones of effort. I've got to admit, I couldn't make head nor tail of it. I don't think the assistive technology I use on my PC helped either in translating the detailed plan. So most of the time I just guessed at what I should do with running, cycling and swimming three times a week. I kind of went by feel, and if I didn't feel up to it then I would do less training or none at all. It was really hit-and-miss when I look back at it. I didn't even have a turbo trainer to use at home, just a normal exercise bike. If I was lucky I would manage to get someone to ride my tandem with me on the weekends, and in the early days I didn't have anyone to run with so just did my runs on the treadmill (affectionately named the dread-mill by most runners), but I didn't really have a choice and I certainly didn't really know what I was doing.

I knew I needed someone to train with, particularly for running if I wanted to start progressing and getting faster. I had heard that my daughter's cello teacher's husband was a good runner, so after a cello concert in early 2009, I plucked up the courage to ask Jane's brother to approach Chris, her husband. Chris Sherwood was busy helping out with the after-concert social gathering and eventually popped across to me and said that he would be more than happy to go out for a run, but he wasn't sure he would be able to keep up. I said that I thought he would be great at it and not to worry. To be honest I wasn't sure I would be able to keep up with Chris, but I needed someone who was speedier than me to ensure they were able to have the lung power to communicate with me on runs, and I was hoping that Chris would fit the bill.

In Chris' own words:

We were chatting over tea and cakes after the end-of-term concert for my wife Jane's cello students, one of whom was Haseeb's daughter Ayeisha. Naturally, having had my ego flattered by the suggestion that I could be faster than the 'other guy', I volunteered.

Chris and I went for our first run and we instantly hit it off and quickly became very close friends. Chris is a vet by profession and he had endless vet stories and pearls of wisdom that he shared with me on runs. Chris, a highly intelligent and funny guy, was a complete natural at guiding. What I really love about him though, above this, is his kindness and sensitivity. Over the coming years he would undoubtedly become one of the best training, racing and generally brilliant friends I have had the pleasure of knowing. I call him 'my brother from another mother'. I never got bored on a run with Chris – the hours flew by and still do when we get the chance to train and chat together. I really missed him during those times when either he or I was injured or for some other reason couldn't train. I know he takes his guiding responsibilities very seriously.

As he puts it:

I take my responsibilities very seriously when running with Haseeb and I am mortified whenever there is a trip, slip, fall or collision. Haseeb is a complete gentleman about these when they happen and is probably quite prepared to lie through his teeth ("Oh, I'm fine!") to save me from feeling completely mortified.

I completed my first triathlon at Woodhall Spar in early 2008. This was a pool-based swim-sprint triathlon (four hundred-metre swim, 20k bike ride and 5k run). The bike leg was completed on my heavy MTB tandem. Nothing to write home about, but I was hooked! I then signed up for my first open-water triathlon, which was a standard-distance race (1,500-metre swim, 40k bike ride and 10k run). Chris recalls the waterlogged race thus:

This was quite the family occasion. Jane and the kids and our friends the Bowen family came along to support, so we had quite a support posse. To say the event was wet was an understatement. Haseeb (bless him) I think had only raced in triathlons with pool-based swims previously and he turned up in an ill-fitting wetsuit more suitable for surfing than swimming. A baggy wetsuit increases drag, slowing you down, and also allows more water in (which makes the wearer colder).

Heavy rain had topped up Grendon Lake with lots of fresh cold water, and with Haseeb's baggy wetsuit we were in the lake for a long time and both came out really cold.

I can't remember much of the bike leg, but we both enjoyed the fact that tandem power allowed us to do plenty of overtaking.

The run was an out-and-back affair with some narrow sections with two-way traffic, not ideal with one fast female athlete slamming hard into Haseeb. The rain continued and by the time the race was finished the registration tent had been taken down to prevent it disappearing into the rising waters of the lake.

Excuse the pun, but 2009 was a watershed year for me. I completed a number of open-water triathlons. I still struggled in the cold water when it came to the open-water races but my strength was definitely showing through in the run. I entered my first paratri race in 2009, guided by Chris. Earlier in the year I invested in a brand-new race tandem, the Landscaper. However, the National Paratri Race was being held in Rother Valley and I heard that the track around the lake was rather muddy and not tarmacked. So, rather than wreck my new tandem I decided to race on my old one. The swim was slow as I expected and the bike section slippery and consequently not particularly fast. Still, my run held together and I came third. Not bad for my first paratri outing. A guy called Iain Dawson finished just behind me and Chris Goodwin came first. These names were going to be very familiar to me in the coming years.

In May of 2009 I was made aware that entries were being accepted for the European Championships in Holten. I recall it being a fraught process, and in those early years everything was handled through the British Triathlon Federation administration. I remember missing the entry deadline, however through some careful negotiation via the BTF, I was allowed to register by the end of May.

So that June I did my first European Championships guided by Chris Sherwood in Holten, Holland. Richard Chipps drove me across with the tandem. It was a real adventure getting there by car as we almost didn't find the B&B Richard had booked. Once we got there it was a fantastic little place 10k outside of Holten. Chris travelled separately, booking into a campsite with his family. It was a relief after all the travelling to finally meet up the day before the race and register. The organisation was incredible, and, being my first major championships, I was just trying to soak up the atmosphere.

Much to my delight it was a particularly hot weekend. This meant that the water temperature was lovely and warm. We did a practice swim the day before the race without wetsuits on and it was lovely and toasty. *Perfect*, I thought.

The excitement mounted on the morning of race day. My only concern was whether Richard would get us to the start line, as he did find the roads rather confusing. Fortunately we left in plenty of time and there was no drama getting there. I got into my wetsuit for my first European Championships and the nerves immediately kicked in. Butterflies in the stomach. We entered the waters for the deep-water start and waited for the hooter to sound.

Once the hooter was sounded, Chris and I got into our rhythm. One of the competitors, Chris Goodwin, came undone from his tether and started to swim in a different direction to his guide. Another competitor had to swim after him and stop him. It was pretty funny. It didn't affect his overall position as he still came out first from the lake. It was no surprise to me that I exited behind the others in fourth place, as my swimming was very weak. Once in transition, Richard whipped off my wetsuit. In those days I was allowed additional help in transition, though later this was not allowed and the guide had to be the athlete's only 'handler'. However, Richard's swift removal of my wetsuit was met with massive cheers from some of the spectators including some female elite triathletes, who then asked Richard, jokingly, whether he would do the same for them to save them valuable transition time in their race!

Once we were on the tandem Chris and I were making good progress. We caught up with an Italian pair, who were in third position. We passed by them quite convincingly. But then disaster struck: the chain came off the bike so we stopped and Chris had to quickly put the chain back on. My heart sank as we were then overtaken by the Italians, knocking us back into fourth position.

We went into our second transition and I got my shoes on and took my helmet off to hear Chris say, "Where is the tether?" It was nowhere to be seen.

Richard, who was standing nearby, improvised and handed us a plastic bag! Good grief, I thought, was I to use a plastic bag as a tether? This wasn't going to help my street cred, for sure. So, there was nothing for it but to use the plastic bag as we started running out of transition.

I then heard Richard call out to us – "I've found the tether!" There was a mighty cheer from the spectators as he handed us the makeshift shoelace tether.

We took a sharp right out of the transition area and started to catch the Italian athlete, who was struggling with his run. We soon overtook them but I knew deep down that there was not a cat in hell's chance of catching the athletes in first and second position. As we approached the end of the run section, just before the finishing shoot, Chris missed the fact that there was a ramp up to the last two hundred metres. Much to his horror, I tripped and fell, grazing my knee. It was going so well up until then! I later found out that all the guides had in fact not noticed the ramp up and therefore tripped all of the visually impaired athletes!

It was my first European race and I got a bronze medal. I was so proud to finish third with my best friend. After we received our medals I asked Chris Goodwin if I could feel his gold medal to see whether it felt any different to my bronze. I'd never really held a medal before. I was so disappointed. I couldn't tell the difference between his medal and mine! It should at least be bigger or heavier or something!

That autumn of 2009 I entered my first half-marathon, again guided by Chris. I was really looking forward to the 13.1 miles around Leicester. Chris and I had been running together for around six months now and we were getting on really well. The trust between the runner and guide is extremely important. The guide does need to be evenly matched to the runner, and if possible much fitter. Being able to think on your feet while guiding someone is a very special skill that not everyone possesses.

Chris and I developed a great method of communication.

He struggled, like most people, with his lefts and rights. So in true Chuckle Brothers style he adopted the relatively foolproof 'to me/to you' school of guiding. The other thing Chris was extremely good at and refined over time was his ability to shout at other runners to move out of the way if they were in front of us or, as quite often happened, runners who passed us by and then cut across us.

I think we learned all of the lessons of the dos and don'ts of guiding at Leicester Half. It was a chilly Sunday morning in October when we hurtled down New Walk at the start of the race. Two minutes into the race and some guy cut across me. His long legs trailed behind and my foot caught his foot. I went flying forwards, head over heels, rolled a couple of times on the hard ground and came to a stop. Chris was horrified. I got back up and noticed that my right gluteal muscle was hurting, but decided to carry on running. We weaved in and out of the other runners. It was pretty tight at times and it wasn't long before my right hand hit a metal fence. Ouch. It was more painful, I think, because of the cold weather. The pain soon subsided and my legs and lungs took their turn in reminding me that they were working hard.

We got to ten miles and I wasn't feeling too bad. I said to Chris that I could step it up if he wanted. Unfortunately Chris had been suffering with a virus so he wasn't able to step up that extra gear. We went through the tricky last three miles, which involved negotiating bollards, curbs, underpasses and the various twists and turns which I find physically and mentally demanding.

We got to the last stretch of the race and Chris said, "Right, let's do a sprint finish." So I ran as hard as I could, but unfortunately both Chris and I went quite wide of each other and I hit the timing post at full pelt. Yes, I had been through the wars in this race.

I ended up in the medical tent with an ice pack strapped to my leg. I also realised a few days later that in the fall I had cracked a rib, and it took me a good six months to recover from that race. I was very pleased with my 1.35 finishing time.

But like a true athlete, I wasn't satisfied with it; I really felt I had a much quicker time in me and a year later I knocked out my first 1.25 half-marathon with Dave Saunders. I was absolutely bowled over. So much so that I remember jumping up, putting my arms around Dave and kissing him on the finish line!

I was interviewed by BBC Radio Leicester, who asked me how the tethering worked. I recall saying something like, "Well, we use a very technical piece of equipment called a shoelace for the tether."

This was a fitting end to an amazing season and I was looking forward to doing a hard block of winter training to prepare myself for what was to come in 2010.

CHAPTER 15

THE GOLDEN YEARS

Having felt that I had completed a relatively satisfactory first season with the GB Squad I was looking forward to a good block of winter training and racing again in the spring. I had joined Leicester Triathlon Club (LTC) again and was doing a number of winter league road races, guided mainly by Chris. However, I knew that I needed to get other guides. This was for a number of reasons. One of these was that I knew that Chris wanted to focus on his own races which I respected. The other reason was that I knew that a faster guide, particularly on the front of my tandem would make a big difference to my overall performance. My coach Richard Chipps introduced me to Andy Foster, a fellow Leicester Triathlon Club member. I remember when he turned up at my house for a training session my wife Mary looked out of the window and said that there was a very young man, tall with blond hair, standing outside. I wondered who she was talking about as I knew Andy was a few years older than me! Maybe this triathlon lark had some rejuvenating effect on those taking it up?

Anyway, Andy was going to be a big influence on my racing over the next year. I did the Markfield 10k Race with Andy, and he remarked towards the end of the race, "Bloody hell, Haseeb, slow down." I did that race in around forty minutes; the quickest race Andy had done in a couple of years.

2010 was another important year for me as it was the first time I took part in the World Triathlon Championships during September in Budapest. As the sport of paratriathlon was in its early years of development it was relatively straightforward to enter races. It was all self-funded too. I did receive a small Sports Aid Fund grant, which helped a little towards equipment and travel, but by and large I spent much more than any funding that came in. I had to pay not only for myself, but for my guide and any support crew.

Before the World Triathlon Championships, earlier that year I competed in my second European Championships. This time it was held in Athlone, Ireland. Now that was something special, and yes, it is true what they say: the Irish certainly know how to put on a party!

In the early years all the paratriathletes had to organise their own travel and accommodation. It's always difficult for me to get this done as it's quite tricky over the internet, so I had to rely upon Mary or Richard to do this on my behalf. It could be quite stressful for them. On this occasion Richard, as with the European Championships the previous year, found some accommodation which seemed to be cheap and would mean that a number of the squad could stay in the same accommodation. This accommodation was a student block just a stone's throw from the starting line. Some of the other squad members jumped at the chance of booking this place and we did this a few months before the race, which took place in June. However, when we got close to the race we had heard nothing from the accommodation manager, so we naturally got worried. Eventually I got hold of him the weekend before. He seemed pretty upbeat and apologised in his lovely Southern Irish accent. He said he couldn't talk long though as he was at a match in Dublin. I think he had been on the Guinness for sure.

So, with the accommodation confirmed we set off for

Athlone in my wife's Vauxhall Zafira. Richard and Andy Foster were both on the insurance so could take it in turns to drive over to Holyhead. We got on the ferry and settled into the journey. There were a number of other paratriathletes also travelling across on the same boat. During the journey I popped to the loo and got locked in. The locking system on the inside of the disabled toilet was some crazy electronic sensor. How anyone blind was supposed to work out how to open the door, God only knows. Anyway, after much banging of my fist against the door a member of crew staff released me from my predicament, only to be greeted by laughter from my GB Team colleagues.

On the ferry I received a call from David Cook, a wheelchair-using para, who had got to the accommodation before us. "Haseeb, is that you?" He sounded really annoyed.

"Er, yes, what's up?"

David complained that he and his wife had had trouble getting into the building. Once in, he found that the apartment was not clean and there was no hot water. I apologised profusely, even though there was nothing I could do about it just then, and said that we would be there later to help sort things out.

Anyway, by the time we arrived, Jane, his wife, had given the place a quick clean and hot water had been restored. I hadn't met Jane before but she was absolutely lovely, softly spoken and small in stature. She had gone the extra mile and cooked up some dinner for us, which was so incredibly nice of her.

Now, we had not only transported my tandem in the car, but Sarah Krishen's (a fellow partially sighted GB triathlete) on the roof rack. We took Sarah's bike off the roof and stored it in the flat and I thought that my tandem would be fine in the car overnight.

The cycle recce for the event was the following morning, but this was to prove extremely stressful indeed. As I got ready for the tandem ride around the bike course, Richard asked me whether he had given me the car key. I said no, he was the last one to have it. The next hour was incredibly stressful as we checked the flat over and over again for the key. All sorts of things went through my mind. The spare key was back in Leicester and there was no way that Mary could get it to me. It was a nightmare. *What happens if we don't find the key?* I was not going to get to race, and getting home would be tricky to say the least.

We were up on the second floor of the student accommodation and the thought had crossed my mind that Richard might have dropped it on the stairs. Andy and Richard went up and down the stairs, checking to see if they could find the key. I could tell that Andy was getting very frustrated as he went extremely quiet. I dreaded to think what might be going through his mind. Richard went back down the stairs again and checked the radiators in the stairwell. He then popped back into the flat and returned jubilant with key in hand. Someone had deposited it on top of one of the radiators. It was a miracle we found the key, to be honest. I was going to race and get back home after all!

The following day Richard had decided to hang up the Leicester Triathlon flag in the window. The flag had the Union Jack on it as well as a number of other international flags. However, the Union Jack was the prominent flag as it often travelled with Leicester Tri members to international races. It wasn't long before the Irish police were knocking on the door, advising us to take the flag down for our own safety. A stark reminder of the fact that even though many bridges had been built in terms of the peace process, the political sensitivities still remain.

Race day arrived and as usual the nerves kicked in. My main memory of the event was the fact that my foot managed to find the only major dip on the course during the run section and I ended up sprawled on the ground. This was becoming a bad habit, falling in races! The run course was very technical with lots of twists and turns in the narrow streets of Athlone. Andy did a sterling job keeping me out of harm's way. However, I was too far behind my GB Team mates and I came third in the end, behind Chris Goodwin and Iain Dawson. Another bronze medal.

That evening we all made our way to a local pub for the incredible post-race party. I was introduced by Richard to some Irish students who were studying in Athlone. One of them was having a birthday party. They seemed mighty impressed with my medal and before I knew it I was persuaded to get on the dance floor. I did have a few rounds and got pretty tipsy. In the meantime, Morgan Williams (British Triathlon staff member, who had done such a superb job supporting the Paratriathlon Squad) was in the other corner of the pub also getting very merry indeed. Other GB guys and girls were in various stages of inebriation, singing and dancing their socks off.

As Andy and I walked back to the accommodation so many locals were shouting, "Well done" to us – it was so lovely, something I will look back on with very fond memories.

In 2010 I was introduced to Duncan Shea-Simonds, a new guide I was to get to know very well over the next few years. Andy Foster was going to race with me in the National Championships at Holme Pierrepont, Nottingham. However, he was doing the John o'Groats to Land's End bike challenge for charity only a week before. He had convinced himself that he was going to be fighting fit for the National Championships. However, when it got close to the championships he had a change of heart and recruited Dunc on my behalf. Andy told me he was really good, one of the best triathletes in the club. I can't remember doing much training with Dunc before the race, I'm pretty sure we only went for a run, so it was really a journey into the unknown for both of us. My first impression of Dunc was of a quiet, very tall and slightly aloof man. There was certainly an enigma about him. He also came across as serious and focused. I had a good feeling that this was a man who raced hard and took no prisoners.

Richard Chipps had got me to Holme Pierrepont and was pretty much providing me with much of the practical support pre-race, so all that was required was to get in the wetsuit, tether up and race. I was nervous about the swim. Would it be cold? If so, then a warm-up was going to be important.

As usual in this particular venue, it was a deep-water start and Dunc and I tethered calf-to-calf. Luckily, I quickly acclimatised to the water, which wasn't too cold, and as we waited my heart started beating faster in anticipation of the starting hooter. Then, boom – we were off. I tried my best to keep my stroke nice and smooth, but it's always tricky in open-water swimming as your arms feel restricted by the neoprene. I had one of the basic Zone3 wetsuits, which wasn't too bad but probably didn't give me the same buoyancy in the water as my more expensive top-of-the-range wetsuits I bought later in my triathlon career.

We came out of the water in second place. I couldn't quite believe it – we were in front of Chris Goodwin, a much better swimmer than I. All I could think was that he must have had some kind of problem, and later found out that a football-sized ball of weed had attached itself to his tether, which slowed him down considerably.

Out of the water, and Dunc and I ran towards the tandem. Dunc pulled down my zip and helped to bring my wetsuit down to my waist. I always find it helpful when my guides assist me by taking my wetsuit down to my waist while on the move. Once in transition Dunc pulled the wetsuit off my bottom half as I dropped to the floor and raised my legs up. Quick and slick. Wetsuit off, and then it was time to stick on the bike helmet, place my hand on my saddle and run alongside the tandem until

I got to the mounting line. My cycle shoes were clipped into the pedals and rubber bands held them in place. Dunc straddled the tandem while I got on and placed my feet in the shoes.

"I'm on!" I shouted, and we both pushed off. We quickly got the tandem going and I started pushing hard on the pedals.

"Keep it smooth, Has," Dunc shouted. I was working so hard that my pedal strokes were clunky as I stamped down with maximum effort on my down strokes.

As we accelerated I couldn't quite believe how fast we were moving. We were taking the corners at around twenty miles per hour. It was both exhilarating and frightening at the same time. I completely trusted Dunc, but kept on thinking that if we hit the deck it wouldn't be a pretty sight. We finished the four-lap twenty-kilometre bike leg in twenty-eight minutes – the fastest 20k I had ever done on a tandem. That would have been an average speed of around twenty-five miles per hour. However, running off the bike wasn't going to be Easy Street, not with Dunc guiding me. Right from the outset Dunc kept on telling me to keep pushing and digging deep. For some this might be really annoying, but for me I find it really helps. I respond well when I'm being constantly encouraged to find as much inner strength and reserve as I can muster. So, I did just that.

I finished in a brilliant second place and received my first silver medal! I now had to concentrate on getting ready for my next big race, the World Championships in September.

The World Championships in Budapest in September 2010 was a wholly different experience for me. For the first time I was about to get a taste of what it was like to badly underperform. Having won silver at the National Championships earlier that year with a new guide, Duncan Shea-Simonds, I was in a buoyant mood. I flew out with Richard Chipps, Chris, my guide, and Mary and my daughter Ayeisha (who was thirteen years old at the time). We arrived three days before the race and checked

Baby Haseeb with Mum and Dad

My family and I in 1988

Haseeb with Mary
and Ayeisha at brother
Toseef's wedding

Chris Sherwood and I, going for bronze at the 2009 European
Paratriathlon Championships

Haseeb and Paratriathlon Team GB with Chrissie Wellington at Training Camp, Summer 2012

Jumping for joy having finished 3rd with guide Ben Matthews at the World Triathlon Championships, London September 2013

Rupert Simms and I tiptoeing through the mud at Wollaton
Park Cross Country Race January 2015

Hand in hand finishing the London Marathon April 2016 with guides Tim Hemming and Ross Welton

Race day at Barcelona Ironman about to go to referee for goggles to be checked

Great swim and on the way to transition to put cycle kit on

Going well on the tandem after 90km of cycling

It feels good to be off the tandem exiting transition to start the
run wearing blacked out goggles

Digging deep during the run with Mary supporting

Suffering like a dog wishing I was somewhere else

into our apartments 10k away from the race start. This was going to prove difficult on race morning.

As soon as we arrived it started to rain, and it didn't stop. I felt so sorry for Mary and Ayeisha as it felt so miserable. They were not keen on coming to support me in races generally, and they would admit openly that they found them boring and in Mary's case quite stressful affairs. So, I felt very guilty that I had dragged them all the way to Budapest for them to get soaking wet and cold.

Richard had persuaded me to leave my race kit with BTF, who were bringing across all the tandems and wheelchairs by land. When we all arrived at the team hotel for race briefing, Richard asked Jonny Riall (the GB manager) whether the tandem and my kit had arrived safely. Jonny said the bike was there but he didn't know anything about the rest of my kit (helmet, bike shoes and trainers). I thought Jonny was joking at first but it quickly dawned on me that he wasn't. My heart just sank. What was I going to do? No helmet, bike shoes or run shoes wasn't exactly good prep for a race.

Some quick thinking and we decided to go buy some new bike shoes and cleats from the expo. Tom Perkins (an arm-impaired paratriathlete) lent me his helmet and Jonny lent me his run shoes despite the fact that they were a size too big (size eight compared to my seven). Well, there was no point moaning or whingeing – I had to get on with it and get ready for the race. The race was extremely early; a 7.30am start, and ideally I like to get to the venue a couple of hours before the race to mentally and physically prepare. We hadn't had a chance to check the cleat positioning on my new bike shoes but that was okay, as long as we got to the transition in the morning with plenty of time in hand.

A bus was organised from our accommodation and we went down to catch it for 6am. Unfortunately the bus driver insisted on waiting as long as he could in case there were any other athletes catching the bus into Budapest. There weren't, but time was running out and some of the athletes started changing on the bus. We got down to the start line on the banks of the Danube at around 6.30; it was so tight and you could feel the tension in the air. I got my wetsuit on and rushed down to transition to set up the rest of my kit. The new bike cleats on my cycle shoes had to be checked, which took some fiddling on the part of Richard. Chris checked his watch. It was 7.25am – only five minutes to get to the start. My heart skipped a beat as he asked a couple of the officials the quickest way down to the race start. We only just arrived in time and had to get into the water, and OMG – it was freezing! My worst nightmare, and no time to warm up or mentally rehearse.

As soon as we got in we had to go. It must have been below fourteen degrees and I just couldn't get my head into the water. I was swimming behind Chris and kept having to stop to calm down and regroup. This was an awful scenario for me. Even without being able to see, I knew I was going to come out of the water last, and I did. It's never a good feeling. There were eight other Visually Impaired (VI) males in the race and I had so much time to make up to catch them. I just got on with the job. We mounted the tandem and I concentrated on putting everything into the bike leg. We were gaining places and overtaking a couple of other athletes and by the time I got to the run my legs were tired.

Getting off the bike and into the run is always a massive challenge and I hadn't quite mastered the art of being able to do it without my legs feeling like lead. I pushed as hard as I could and managed to claw back another place. So I didn't finish last, which was my aim after the disappointing swim. Still, it was disappointing; I just knew I had more to give and it hadn't happened on this day. Things could only get better, however, and as this was my last triathlon of the season I could look back and see plenty of positives to take forward from my year of racing!

2011 was a great year for me in respect of triathlons and in completing my first marathon. The year kicked off to a stonking start. I asked Duncan to guide me in a six-mile race in Barrow, Leicestershire. The race was in January but the conditions were good and in those days my taper (decreasing training in the run up to a competition) consisted of no training for a whole week before a race; so I rested up and conserved some energy.

Come race day Dunc and I rocked up to the start and we set off at a very brisk pace – the first mile was 5.20 minutes. Wow, I didn't think I could keep that up, and as expected my speed did go down a bit but the next mile was still under six minutes. Every mile hurt more than the last as my lungs felt like they were exploding, but I kept going. The ground was fairly even so I didn't have to worry too much about any trip hazards. All in all, four of my six miles were under the six minutes per mile pace.

When we crossed the finishing line Dunc was really happy – "Mate, we knocked off 35.42!" I couldn't believe it. Going at that pace you really need a competent guide who knows what they are doing. Dunc was brilliant throughout, letting me know when a dip was coming up, alerting me to turns and twists, and telling me to shorten my stride going up the couple of hills on the course. Having someone like Dunc by my side guiding me brings out the best in me and allows me to relax while running.

I have never managed to go that quickly since – maybe there is something in adopting a pre-race strategy of not training for days before a race. In truth, I think the real reason was that I was very light at the time, around fifty-four kilos, which is about eight stone and eight pounds. Everything must have fallen into place at the right time and I was lucky enough to peak for that race. Also, as mentioned Dunc has a habit of really pushing me beyond my perceived limits, a pattern which was to continue over the years. I still didn't really know Dunc all that well at this point yet, he was still able to get the best out of me. Dunc has a very distinctive approach to guiding. For him when it is obvious that I am beginning to flag during a race he has no qualms about shouting at me constantly in order to raise my game. It works! This was in contrast to other guides who would have seen that I was suffering may have felt sorry for me and allowed me to step off the gas a little.

In March I was guided by Dunc who again gave me a proper beasting in the Ashby Twenty-Mile Race. I finished this in two hours seventeen minutes. This was a great time but I was absolutely smashed at the end. My legs had serious delayed onset muscle soreness (DOMS) and I developed a problem with both calves.

The London Marathon was five weeks later and I was hoping to do a three-hour marathon. Unfortunately for me, my lack of previous racing at this level was to be the determining factor in my performance in this race. Dunc and I went down to London and stayed at his sister's house. Hannah and her husband really looked after us well. The drive down was really nice as this was one of the rare opportunities for me to talk to Dunc. I think we covered a number of topics including religion and family. For me, at any rate, it's extremely important to get to know my guides on another level than just turning up and racing. There is a tremendous amount of emotional investment we put into working together as a team. I place my life in their hands, literally, and building a meaningful relationship is something I feel I can give back to my guides, and of course, close friends who have supported me over the years.

So, Dunc and I went out for a little training run the day before the London Marathon and I could still sense that I hadn't quite recovered from the Ashby Twenty-Mile Race.

When we registered for the race what we didn't realise

was that we had been given different pens. An administrative oversight. I was in Pen 9, which was five pens down from where Dunc had been placed. We tried to ask the officials to place us in a higher pen but they just weren't listening to Dunc or me. We were getting nowhere, but had to sort this out fast otherwise we were going to end up with the much slower runners, having to fight through massive crowds. This would have put paid to my attempt at a three-hour marathon. Some quick thinking and we went to the information point to try to get some help. The head marshal saw sense and placed us both in Pen 4 and we were then able to relax and enjoy the carnival atmosphere.

Prior to the race we were hoping that Jonathan Edwards would interview us, after all I, a blind athlete, was going for a sub-three-hour marathon. We were asked by Jonathan's TV crew to stand and wait while he interviewed one person after another in fancy dress costumes but he never came across to us. Dunc has never forgiven Jonathan for this snub and I am reliably informed that he says a few choice words every time he appears on telly. Dunc has joked that next time we do London he will dress up like a guide dog to get a TV interview!

Once in the pen we waited to shuffle forward after the countdown. I just couldn't believe the number of people surrounding us. This was going to be very tricky for Dunc guiding me, and for me in terms of various trip hazards.

Once we got going I felt in control until we got to mile fifteen. Up until this point there was the usual dodging of people on the course, bottles to avoid slipping on and idiots with headphones in their ears who couldn't hear Dunc telling them to get out of the way. However, when I got to mile fifteen something happened. I started to feel dizzy and disorientated; looking back I was possibly dehydrated. Also, my niggles started to surface and the issues I had with my calves began to magnify. It was tough, and I said to Dunc that I didn't know whether I could continue. Dunc just said that he hadn't come all this way for me to walk the marathon (classic Dunc), so I resolved to do what I could to keep myself going. I felt so bad and guilty that I couldn't run any quicker but I kept going nonetheless.

Our time suffered, and I finished in a disappointing three hours forty-two minutes. I understand this is a time most people would be so happy with but I knew I was quicker than that on paper. In hindsight I think this was a very important lesson for me. I was just so complacent, assuming that I could rock up and smash out a three-hour marathon or better on my first attempt. I realised that I needed to do a lot more training and get my legs accustomed to marathon training which would take time and patience.

However, once my legs had recovered from the London Marathon experience, the fitness I had built up proved to have a positive impact on the 2011 triathlon season. The National Paratriathlon Championships were coming up in the next couple of months, which was enough time for me to recover from the marathon. I'd been getting plenty of swim coaching from Richard and my biking was coming on.

The championships were held at Holme Pierrepont in Nottingham, which is known to be a fast course. Again Dunc was guiding me for this race and I knew he was on good form. However, it was my swim that I was worried about. We decided to tether waist-to-waist instead of calf-to-calf for this event, so I swam behind Dunc, allowing for smoother turning around buoys and less tangling of arms.

We had to swim up to the swim start, which suited me just fine as it allowed me to warm up. When we got going I felt really good. My arms were turning quickly and I just felt that Dunc and I had connected and were in sync. I couldn't believe my ears when Dunc said that we were just behind Iain Dawson, who was the current world champion. I knew then that I was in real contention to win the race.

On the tandem we were only fifty seconds behind Iain and his guide. I didn't worry too much about this as I knew my run was much quicker than Iain's, and indeed on the run I quickly caught and overtook him. But as we negotiated some traffic cones, disaster struck when my foot clipped one of these and I went flying.

As I hit the deck I heard Iain saying to his guide, "What happened?"

His guide said, "Don't worry, it's just Has falling over."

I got back up and carried on running and overtook Iain again. I crossed the finishing line a good fifty seconds in front of him. I was absolutely elated. I hugged Dunc and kissed him on the cheek. My first gold medal!

"We did it, buddy, we did it!"

It took a long while for the BTF to make up their minds to invite me to the World Championships in Beijing, but I got the call. It was amazing. I was going to fly to Beijing with Dunc and everything was going to be paid for. This was the first time the BTF had financed athletes to participate in an international race. I was, however, a bit nervous about going all that way and spending considerably more time with Dunc than I had previously. I had only spent a little bit of time with him when he drove us down to London earlier that year.

In previous triathlon races, I always had someone like Richard supporting me with the day-to-day stuff like getting around hotels, helping in the restaurants or just with the logistics of getting ready for the race. I had got to know Richard really well and felt utterly relaxed around him. We had a laugh and a joke and felt completely at ease in each other's company. I didn't worry about asking Richard for help and never felt as though he resented giving me support, and he always kept his notorious untidiness to his side of the hotel room.

I was told by the GB Team management that I wasn't allowed

an additional helper in Beijing. If I wanted someone then I would have to pay for them myself, which I couldn't afford. I was going to be wholly reliant on Dunc, who I didn't feel I knew very well at this time. I wasn't sure how he was going to cope with or feel about this. For me it is so important that the person supporting me is happy to do so and doesn't mind being with me for lengthy periods. It can be very stressful for the helper or guide, and it is tough for me too. I am out of my comfort zone in a completely alien environment. Back home I know where everything is. In my house everything is kept in the same place so I can find things easily. I go out with my guide dog to places my dog and I are familiar with. In other words, at home I am very independent. When I go to places I don't know I become wholly reliant upon the person I am with. It can be incredibly frustrating for me to not be able to leave my hotel room without help, or be able to get my own breakfast, for instance.

So, when we eventually got to Beijing and booked into the hotel I was aware that Dunc was finding my ongoing support needs a challenge. To his credit, he didn't say anything to me. I wanted him to be able to pop off and do his own thing in order for him to have his own space. Dunc is a very quiet kind of guy, and many folk would say that he is as hard as nails. Yet, the more I got to know him, I discovered a very sensitive side to him, which I'm sure he won't thank me for mentioning. Despite the amount of stress this situation caused Dunc, he did look after me very well, and we got on just fine. I remember going to the Chinese Walmart with Dunc and picking up some dragon fruit. When we got it back to the hotel room Dunc very carefully peeled and diced it for me. He is a very kind and caring human being who I have grown to respect and admire beyond his incredible athletic abilities.

It wasn't long before race day crept up on us. The swim was in a reservoir and, as I had found out the day before during swim practice, surprisingly warm. The weather overall wasn't overly warm, a comfortable twenty degrees or so. Dunc and I had decided that I wouldn't go wetsuit-free, as the buoyancy of the wetsuit often helps lift me higher in the water and gives me an advantage that I sorely need in the swim. However, once the hooter had sounded and we were off, I felt too warm. I just couldn't get into the same groove as I did in the National Championships. I knew my time would be down compared to what it was earlier that year, and indeed I came out of the water in around fourteen minutes. I was in third place.

On to the tandem leg, and it was a double loop of the bike course, which included a nasty little hill towards the beginning. This meant getting out of my saddle and giving it some real welly. There is a great photo of me pushing hard on the back of the tandem on this hill.

We took a sharp left-hand turn, and as we did I just about heard Dunc say, "Iain Dawson is out of the race!"

I couldn't quite believe what I had just heard. Ian was in second place at this point. "What?" I asked.

"Iain's out – concentrate, Has," Dunc replied. So I tried to keep the pedalling as smooth as I could and focused on my own race. Later I found out that Iain and his guide Liam had overshot the corner and crashed into a wall. Fortunately they only suffered minor cuts and bruises.

Once on to the run, the gap between me and the Brazilian in first place was around one and a half minutes. I ran as hard as I could but I knew I couldn't catch him. I knocked out a respectable eighteen minutes for the run and finished in silver position, not bad for my second World Championships.

Dunc and I were able to relax now. It was nice to do a bit of sightseeing (well, for Dunc anyway) and experience a little bit of real Chinese life. We had only been allowed English cuisine up until this point but Dunc and I asked the chef to cook us up some authentic local cuisine. It was absolutely fantastic. We also visited the Great Wall of China and local tombs of past emperors.

One day we went for a bike ride to spin out the legs. Spinning out the legs basically means going for a fairly easy bike ride to help the legs recover from a hard race. It gets the blood flowing through the muscles which helps with speedier recovery. So, we were cycling away from our accommodation on a fairly straight road when I heard Dunc swear loudly, and then almost simultaneously the tandem swerved, mounted a pavement and I heard the screams of young children, who were frantically running away from the oncoming tandem. I later learned, when Dunc had calmed down enough to communicate it to me, that an oncoming car was overtaking another motor vehicle, and was heading straight in our direction. We were about to have a headlong collision with this car when Dunc narrowly avoided certain death by taking the tandem off the road. Later he commented that if I hadn't been so light he wouldn't have been able to manoeuvre the tandem as well as he did and we would have done the rest of our triathlons in Heaven (and I don't think he was talking about Hawaii).

As much as I enjoyed going to Beijing, a truly once-in-a-lifetime experience, it was lovely to get back home. I always get homesick eventually and getting back to my familiar surroundings and being reunited with my loved ones and independence is truly wonderful. However, it wasn't long before I was jet-setting off to another race. This time I was to be guided by my good friend Rupert Simms. Another adventure awaited.

CHAPTER 16

CLASSIFICATION, A DEAD BIRD AND THE PARALYMPIC PROGRAMME

My very last race of 2011 was the World Duathlon Championships in Gijón, Northern Spain with my good friend Rupert Simms guiding me. What a little adventure this was. At Stansted Airport as we waited on the plane Rupert could see our tandem in its box being loaded on, and then taken off. He thought it odd and asked the air hostess if everything was okay. She reassured us that the tandem would be loaded onto the other side of the aircraft.

However, once we got to Spain and waited for our luggage and tandem, neither had turned up. Clearly the hostess had told us what we wanted to hear to avoid any potential in-flight issues. We arrived on the Wednesday and were due to race on Saturday. As Thursday came and went, then Friday, I really thought I wasn't going to be able to race. However, as if by some miracle, the tandem arrived on the morning of the race. Rupert built the bike as quickly as he could. There was a small technical issue with the headset of the tandem, but the mechanic assigned to the GB Team said we could race on it.

I finished in third place behind two partially sighted guys. We had been held up in the second transition by a fellow GB athlete getting in the way due to the transition area being incredibly tight. I'm sure we would have come second otherwise, but that's racing for you – things can get messy. Both Rupert and I were delighted to get bronze. Apart from the racing we had a lovely time exploring the local town and savouring the wonderfully rich and flavoursome food. I so love going to areas of the world I probably would never think of visiting if it wasn't for the racing. I get a great deal from tasting the local food, smelling the wonderful fragrances around me (not just food smells!) and listening to the different sounds of the places around me.

2012 was pretty uneventful in terms of triathlons. I decided not to enter the European Championships as they were being held in Israel. Furthermore, we had to self-finance again and I just couldn't afford it, and in a way, this was not a bad time to take a bit of a break. My wife and daughter were getting fed up of all the time I was spending travelling and away from home. I still entered the World Duathlon Championships in Nancy, France with Rupert, where I came fourth. This was disappointing as I hoped to do one better than the previous year, but I hadn't been well in the lead-up to the race. Nonetheless, Rupert and I had the customary wonderful time savouring the local delicacies. Boy, the French know how to cook good food.

Now, Rupert Simms is someone I have gotten to know extremely well over the past few years and I can say without hesitation that he is a very close personal friend. Rupert is someone I feel utterly at ease with, find easy to talk to, and is incredibly knowledgeable on conservation matters. He had been piloting my tandem on and off for a couple of years and we had raced together, as mentioned previously. There are a couple of highly amusing tandem-riding stories I will never forget.

One day we were riding towards Foxton Locks. When we got near the canal he spotted a bronze life size statue of a working pony and his charge (a young boy walking next to the pony).

"Hey, Haseeb, I'll take you down to have a feel of this statue

– it's pretty life-size, I think you will appreciate it." We went down and I had a feel of the ornate structure – I should add that this is how I interpret things around me; I find touch a useful and powerful method of interpreting the world. Rupert then suggested that we take the towpath back to Leicester.

"Are you sure, mate? Is there enough space on the footpath?" I asked. Rupert assured me there was and that he had done the trip numerous times.

However, it became very clear that the footpath wasn't as wide as he thought in places, and parts had tree roots coming up through the ground so it was very bumpy. We got to a section where it was extremely muddy and the tow path sloped heavily down towards the canal. I felt the tandem starting to slip down in the direction of the canal water, and suddenly we found ourselves knee deep in the canal! Fortunately we didn't go in any deeper and were able to pull the tandem back on to the path. This has become one of my most popular funny stories, to Rupert's horror/delight.

On another occasion Rupert stopped the tandem on a long ride in the countryside.

"Hey, Haseeb, I've just seen some roadkill, I think it's a pheasant." So he got off the tandem, walked back and picked it up. The bird was still warm and to ensure it was put out of its misery he twisted its neck. Unfortunately, Rupert accidently pulled the poor bird's head off.

"Oh no!" he exclaimed. "Have you got any string so that I can tie it to the tri-bars on the tandem?"

"No," I replied, "I don't really carry around string just in case we need to tie dead pheasants to my tandem."

Rupert improvised and used his scarf to tie the dead bird to my tandem and we cycled home! He told me later that he had the bird for dinner a week later and it was delicious. I didn't get a morsel!

I asked Rupert to share his experience of how we first met

and his perspective of guiding me, and this is what he has written:

At the age of fourteen I joined Beacon Cycling Club in Birmingham and began what was to become a highly sporadic cycle-racing career. One of the regular riders on our Sunday club runs was a blind man named Colin, who was piloted on a tandem by one or two of the men. Colin and I exchanged a few words from time to time but I never really got to know him. I was a little shy and awkward and he never made eye contact. However, I did come to appreciate that the tandem was the perfect vehicle for fresh air and hard exercise for someone in Colin's situation and I know he got great pleasure from those Sunday-morning rides, even in the depths of winter.

At the time I thought it would have been rude to try and muscle in on the piloting rota and I wasn't sure that I could handle either the tandem or the responsibility, but resolved that if I ever got the chance to pilot a blind rider in the future I would take it.

Throughout my late teens and early twenties I was distracted from competitive cycling by a combination of sex, drugs and rock-climbing, in more or less that order, and it wasn't until my thirties that, having started a family and feeling the need to get properly fit again, I decided to join Leicester Road Cycling Club. Not long afterwards I received an email from Haseeb's coach asking for training partners for a blind triathlete. I had done a couple of sprint-distance triathlons and quickly realised that being relied upon by a blind person would not only force me to get out more but could be a useful trump card against family obligations. I was thrilled to get a prompt reply and after a brief chat on the phone with the man himself, made a date.

A few days later I found myself at Haseeb's house watching with interest the way he moved around his own home with ease, almost as if he could see. Later when my children met Haseeb they were bowled over by this and began to question whether he was actually blind. Although I'd never met a blind person in this situation before, I more or less knew what to expect.

What I didn't expect was what happened next: "Okay, shall we go for a ride then?" he said within less than two minutes of my arrival. I was taken aback. I knew that this was what I'd come for but I'd assumed there would be some kind of vetting, or the setting out of ground rules before, perhaps, a tentative spin round the block. I had thought perhaps Haseeb's coach Richard would be there to give me the once-over and check that I was what and who I said I was, but after a quick saddle adjustment at my end we were off down the A6 with no clear plan, and peeled off onto country lanes as soon as the opportunity arose.

This was a joy beyond my expectations. For a few years I'd cycled around the rolling Leicestershire countryside occasionally, but usually alone. Here was someone I'd met for the first time who was easy company and with lots to say. We had a surprising amount in common besides a love of cycling and now we were setting off into the world, taking each turn as it came. Haseeb's swanky racing tandem was easier to handle than I'd feared it would be, although not without its challenges; I was in control and we were both safe.

Haseeb, of course, had done this before and gave me a quick run-down of the things I needed to give advance warning of: when we needed to stop or make a sharp turn, when hills loomed and so on. This would allow him to prepare and make fine adjustments, leaning into corners or easing off on the pedals before I changed gear. We still do more or less the same thing although these days less is said out loud; either Haseeb picks up on subtle cues from me or just goes along with what I'm doing. This is a good thing. It's best not to have to speak too much whilst racing as it can create an impression that I'm not trying hard enough, and although sometimes rehearsing guiding prompts prior to a race can be useful, especially whilst running, as a rule less is better. Ease of communication and an awareness of what the other is thinking or doing is of course one of the pleasures of getting to know someone well. That said, I have been spotted inadvertently walking Haseeb into delicately stacked shop displays and he doesn't always make it cleanly through doorways when we're out together.

Suddenly there was the sound of metal breaking from behind me. Feeling the bike pull to one side, I swerved, hanging on the handlebars this way and that to wrestle back control. I had to stop, but reaching for the brakes meant loosening my grip on the bars and that could put us both on the tarmac. I managed to pull over, put my foot down and wondered whether we would be able to get home without being rescued – the shame of it!

I was confused. Something had gone seriously wrong with the bike but the wheels hadn't locked up, the chain was still on and the wheels seemed intact. As I turned and dismounted, Haseeb informed me his handlebars had come loose. That was it! The rear handlebars on a tandem are fixed to the pilot's seat post. When I had adjusted the saddle before setting out I'd also been thoughtful enough to adjust the rear handlebars to the correct height, but hadn't noticed the metal collar that protected the carbon fibre seat post and allowed the handlebars to grip. Twenty miles into the ride the whole lot had come loose and nearly led to disaster.

Having set off without tools, there was no way I could rectify the problem and we had to make the journey home with completely loose rear handlebars. It was a nervous ride for me but Haseeb didn't seem that bothered, even when he had to grip my seat post to make it safely around corners. It was a relief when we finally got back in one piece and to my surprise Haseeb wanted to arrange to do much the same thing the following week. We've been riding together ever since, and although as I'm writing this it's been a couple of months since our last trip I'm very much looking forward to the next one.

I have also been lucky enough to get to know a number of brilliant people who over the past few years have helped me out so much with my training tandem-riding, swimming and running. I will be forever grateful to my training buddies. I can't name them all but feel the need to mention Ian Abson, Julian Hacket, Ollie Hatton, Dan Leak, Joshua Cardwell, Nicola Rossell, Nini Ratanaporn, James McCall and Dan Leak. All of whom I have had the pleasure and fun of getting to train with, and developing valuable friendships.

Now, someone else I owe a debt of gratitude to is my sports therapist Brian Burrows. I wouldn't ordinarily pay someone to inflict pain on me, but Brian is definitely an exception to that rule. I was recommended to Brian and made an appointment to see him. Little did I know that my appointment, which I thought was going to be for an hour, would turn into a three-hour complete and utter body overhaul. To say that Brian does a thorough job is a massive understatement. So, while you're being manipulated into positions you didn't think your poor old body could possibly manage, Brian asks you some deep, meaningful question. You go quiet, not because you don't want to answer the question but because by merely opening your mouth you think you may just let out a very large scream! Yet, going to see Brian has been one of the best things I ever did and there are very few therapists out there I would trust as much as Brian. Besides which, I consider him to be one of the most trustworthy friends I have.

Back to racing, and in 2012 I had entered the Chester Marathon being held in the autumn. I so wanted to get close to or under three hours for 26.2 miles. I had been training hard with Chris Sherwood over the summer and I was really feeling that the training was paying off.

Chris and I left the day before the race in his camper van and we stayed at a campsite that Chris had very kindly booked in advance. It was a lovely evening and we had packed one of my mum's awesome curries. Man, my mum's curries are phenomenal, and to top it off we then popped into a pub for a drink and pudding. In those days I always thought it important to carb-load before a big race. It sort of worked for me, although I understand that there are some purists out there who would disagree with my choice of pre-race nutrition.

On race day, it was a little chilly in the morning as we gathered in the pen. The grass was still a little wet from the evening dew but it was a lovely morning to be honest, perfect marathon weather. We bumped into another blind guy and his guide. We got into a conversation and they said that they were aiming to finish in around three hours and seven minutes. I said we were going for slightly quicker, and I could sense that the VI runner wasn't impressed, as there was a long pause after I had expressed our intent. I got the impression he wanted to run a quicker time than me. That was okay – the feeling was mutual as I wanted to beat him too! Yes, it was good to have a little bit of competition.

As we set off and passed the undulating grass section we quickly got onto nice open road. The course wasn't exactly flat, as it had been sold to us, but nor was it too hilly. Sections of the course stretched into Wales and Chris told me that the countryside was very scenic. Halfway through I said to him that it would be good to finish in front of the other VI runner and his guide. I asked Chris if he had seen them and he didn't reply. In fact, he told me later that we were just behind them but he didn't want to raise my expectations.

I indicated to Chris that I could step up the pace if he was up to it. Chris wasn't feeling confident at this point, so said that if we both felt good at twenty miles then we could treat the last twenty miles as a 10k race. Eventually we reached the twenty-mile point and I told Chris I was feeling really strong and suggested we could up the pace. He told me that he couldn't run any quicker so I relaxed and settled into a steady trot. I must admit that it was a little frustrating for me as I knew I had plenty more reserves in the tank. The last couple of miles were going to be even more difficult for Chris. His calves started to seize up with cramp and he slowed down significantly.

We finished in a very respectable time of three hours eight minutes. The other good news was that we beat the other blind guy by a large margin, and yes, it felt good! My competitive nature always gets the better of me on these occasions. However, I was still disappointed that the sub-three-hour marathon was so close but so far. Although eight minutes doesn't seem a lot, just that extra couple of seconds per mile make a massive difference in respect of pacing.

2012 was of course an amazing year for another reason. The Olympics and Paralympics came to London. I got a chance to go down and spectate at the triathlon, which took place in Hyde Park. I have to say it was an incredible experience. Although I couldn't obviously see what was happening, the atmosphere was electric. When Alistair Brownlee came storming into the finish and grabbed the GB flag it sent tingles running down my spine; it was utterly awesome. I felt a sense of pride and it filled me with the hunger and desire to never stop reaching out to be the best I could be.

The Olympic Games brought with them some sensational performances from many of the Olympians from across our beautiful planet. All inspirational in their own right, but of course, I had my own personal heroes including Mo Farah, Jessica Ennis-Hill and the Brownlee brothers. What really took me by surprise, though, was how the Paralympics took the country by the scruff of the neck and said, "Hello, world, we are every bit as good as our Olympian brothers and sisters." The only sadness I had was the fact that the Paratriathlon wasn't included this time around. However, plans were afoot to work with the International Paralympic Committee to pull together a strategy which would ensure, for the first time, inclusion of my sport for the 2016 Rio games.

I also had the opportunity to soak in the atmosphere down in the Olympic Park and witness the swimming heats. Again, it was a wonderful experience and I was so happy with the level of genuine public interest in the Paralympics and the many hard-working and dedicated Paralympians. I hoped that one day I would join them and become a Paralympian myself. Granted, I would be forty-six years old but if I could be given the right support I knew that I could improve and put in the hard graft needed to take me to the next level.

2013 was interesting from the classification point of view. In previous years the International Triathlon Union (the international governing body for triathlons) had stipulated that all visually impaired athletes had to wear blacked-out glasses for the run. They didn't have to wear these for the swim or bike legs, just the run. This was extremely unpopular with the partially sighted athletes, as they felt that the little vision that they had, which they used during races, would be taken away from them and put them at risk. In fact, one of the American partially sighted triathletes was taking legal action against his national federation, arguing that he was being discriminated against. I, on the other hand, wasn't disadvantaged at all because it made no difference to me, being totally blind already. Whilst I had sympathy with my fellow VI athletes my view has always been that to level the playing field the ITU should split the highly competitive VI male category into those with partial sight and those who are totally blind. To my utter amazement, in late spring this is exactly the decision the ITU took.

I wasn't expecting to be included in the GB Squad, to be perfectly frank. However, I applied and, to my shock, I got a call-up to compete in the European Championships in Turkey. I approached Ben Matthews, a young triathlete from Loughborough University, to guide me for that season. Ben stepped up and we did a couple of sprint-distance races before the European Championships. He seemed a pretty cool guy and we got on well. We hooked up and arranged a couple of training sessions.

Unfortunately in April 2013, during the National Duathlon Championships at Prestwold Hall, Loughborough, guided by a super-strong athlete by the name of David Gorley, I broke my toe. I had just dismounted from the bike and we were running through transition. I had my hand on the back seat running next to the tandem, and as we turned the corner my foot connected very hard with someone's prosthetic limb. The pain was excruciating! David asked me if I was all right. Even though I wasn't, I didn't want to let on that my toes felt like they were on fire. I carried on running on a very painful foot. The adrenaline and heat of the race helped me to push through to the end and smash out a personal best and bank a silver medal.

I went to A&E two weeks later and the X-ray confirmed the fracture. No running for eight weeks for me. This was certainly a setback, as I had no idea whether I would recover in time for the European Championships. So, it was into the pool for plenty of aqua-jogging and a huge dose of faith.

In June 2013, Ben Matthews and I made the journey out to Alanya. Richard Chipps also joined us for much-needed practical support and it certainly made life much easier. Richard ensured that I got to where I needed to go, helped at dinner times and assisted with getting me and my kit to the required locations.

As it was so warm he made me test my urine every day, as directed by the team doctor. "Come on, Haseeb, pee into this bottle," he would say.

"Are you taking the piss again, Richard?" I would reply. Richard and I had a great banter going between us. I really enjoyed spending time with him, such a great guy.

Race day was hot. This was my first experience of a race in temperatures of over twenty-five degrees. I was very worried about the sea swim. Ben Matthews and I had practised swimming in the sea a couple of days before the race. It was very choppy and I felt myself being thrown around as if I was in a washing machine – a sensation I didn't enjoy, and it made me feel a little sick. But the more I swam, the better I was able to ignore the turbulent waters. However, come race day I need not have concerned myself. The swim was in a sheltered bay and it was completely flat. Nonetheless, my swim wasn't great and once again my technique let me down. However, the bike leg proved to be strong and my run held up and I came third in the PT6A category for totally blind male paratriathletes.

Now, the issue of classification is always a thorny subject. At this point, all of the GB paratriathletes were asked to get classified by a qualified ophthalmologist. I am assuming that all other national federations required their VI athletes to do the same. However, there was no consistency of approach or standard applied. For Paralympic classification, there are two classifiers who classify visually impaired athletes but this bit was missing from the process. So, basically I was competing against some of the partially sighted males who should have been in a different category to myself. Some of these guys were reclassified later in 2014 but for now, they were competing as totally blind competitors and finishing ahead of me.

The difficulty with this comes down to the fact that for me as a blind athlete, the practical challenges and barriers I face trying to train were never acknowledged. For example, I can never run hands-free on a treadmill having to hold on with one hand, swimming in the pool without being able to see the black line is very tough and not being able to see the computer on a Wattbike means that I have to be assisted here too. I remember having a conversation with one of the partially sighted athletes who wondered how I could swim in a straight line without seeing the black strip on the bottom of the pool. Some of the partially sighted guys, for instance, can ride a solo bike by themselves, compete by themselves and require very little support when getting out and about.

This did wind up some of my guides over the years. I remember one or two of them saying, "Has, that guy isn't blind! He's watching TV, mate. He can see."

Of course, it's never that simple and I wouldn't want to suggest that anyone was cheating and wasn't sight impaired, but for anyone reading this, you will start to understand the complexities and difficulties in making the sport a level playing field. This became even more of an issue when the International Triathlon Union (ITU) brought in factoring in 2014. The bottom line is that there is a distinct lack of consistency in classifying athletes and introducing a system which is fair. I much preferred splitting the visually impaired category between those who are partially sighted and those who are blind. The rest is down to the classifiers to ensure that there is a robust system in place to ensure people are in the right categories.

In 2013 the World Championships were in London. This meant only a short trip in a bus down to London and having the home advantage. There is nothing like racing in a World Championships on your own doorstep. Ben and I set off for holding camp in Loughborough before travelling down to London on the minibus with the rest of the GB Squad. It was a great feeling having all the squad together with all of the support staff around. We were all buzzing and excited about travelling down. I was sat next to a friend who had volunteered to help Ben and me out in London, happily chatting away, not realising that

I was perhaps talking a tad too loudly and keeping other folk from their naps until the team manager told me to put a cork in it. This is a bad habit I have, and another one of my friends who helped me out at a training camp a year later had told his wife that every time he started to nod off in the apartment I would pipe up and ask him a question and he never managed to get any kip. I obviously had no idea he was shutting his eyes in preparation for the much-needed break from me.

The race was to take place in Hyde Park; a wonderful setting for what was to be a spectacular event. I got my wetsuit on and tucked my long, curly hair into my swim hat. Coming out of the water I had no idea what position I was in. I knew that Ben and I were making excellent progress on a very fast course. I could hear familiar voices shouting and cheering us on. It was so exciting. Once on the run, again it was hard to know which position we were in. Chris Goodwin, I knew, would be in front. He had a great guide, Ben Howard, who was an ex-pro elite triathlete. My guide Ben Matthews told me that there was someone in front and we were catching them. We literally had another four hundred metres to go and I pushed hard. We overtook the Slovenian pair in front of us and around two minutes later we were crossing the finishing line in bronze position. I was so incredibly happy that I jumped up and did a little jig. This iconic image of me was captured on film and posted on the BTF's website.

That evening the BTF organised a celebratory meal. It started off as a very civilised affair, a three-course meal with plenty of wine being poured. I admit I had quite a bit to drink but was well in control, unlike some of the guides and paratriathletes who ended up pretty hammered. One of the guides escorted me out of the building and the idea formed that we would go on to find other places to drink or a club, after all, the night was young.

I'm not sure how the next bit happened but one of the guides thought it would be a great idea if another visually impaired GB Team member guided me, so I got handed over. The blind-drunk blind teammate was so drunk he was swaying and slurring his words. Anyway, he was more than happy to take over guiding duties, and he told me not to worry as he could follow the white line along the concourse outside the Imperial College refectory building. The rain was lashing down and as we paused to work out what we were going to do next, I decided to, just like in the TV programme *Who Wants to Be a Millionaire*, call a friend to rescue me from possible peril.

The medal ceremony was held the following day in Trafalgar Square. Some GB Team members were feeling rather tender from the celebrations of the previous evening. I felt absolutely fine, although when I got onto the stage I turned to shake hands with my fellow athletes and almost fell off the stage! Ben Matthews grabbed my arm and just about stopped me from breaking my neck.

Despite the ups and downs of these championships I was still mighty proud of my achievements. I had fought hard to get to the championships and clawed back places during the race to podium once more. Yes, it was a good feeling and one I shared with family and friends who came to watch. This was the last big competition of 2013 and an opportunity to take a month of training and enjoy some downtime.

2014 was an amazing year for me for several reasons. The first bit of good news was that somehow I managed to wind up on the World Class Paratriathlon Programme. This was the Paralympic National Lottery-funded programme to assist the GB paratriathletes with training and paying for things like coaching, sports massage and anything to enable the athletes to maximise their performance. It wasn't a lot, to be fair, but it helped. I had received a small amount of Sports Aid funding in the past which did help with supporting me in my sport, but this was on another level altogether. The lottery funding also helped the BTF with the purchase of equipment and paying for training camps. All very necessary if the GB Team was going to be successful in the Paralympic Games in Rio in 2016.

The beginning of 2014 was, however, dominated by preparation for my sub-three-hour attempt at the London Marathon. Going under three hours is the Holy Grail for many long-distance runners and I was no different in that respect. So, I started my tough regime of five runs a week plus some biking and swimming to continue with the triathlon-specific sports to help with injury prevention. The big question was, would I break the three-hour barrier in April 2014?

CHAPTER 17

THE HOLY GRAIL: RUNNING A SUB-THREE MARATHON

The beginning of 2014 was dominated by training for my sub-three-hour marathon attempt. I needed a fast guide who could be guaranteed to run under three hours. It didn't matter if I couldn't quite dip under the three-hour mark, but the plan was to bust out a 2.59.59 marathon, so I wanted to make sure that if I was on form it wouldn't be my guide who didn't have the legs for it. I had, through the help of my coach sending out a tweet, been introduced to a new guide by the name of Rodger Wilkins. Rodger lived in Blackburn, so getting together with him prior to London for a training run was going to be tricky. I had a few telephone conversations with Rodge and he sounded like a lovely guy. He certainly gave me the impression that he wasn't going to let me down.

In Rodge's own words, he eloquently describes our meeting and friendship:

I've had the pleasure of meeting a handful of upbeat, engaging, funny and seriously determined individuals in my time, but none quite like Haseeb Ahmad.

We crossed paths – literally, ha-ha (as Haseeb would write!) – in April 2014 just two days before I attempted to guide him around the London Marathon.

A few weeks earlier I'd responded to a tweet: Anybody fancy joining a 3 man "guiding team" for blind runner Haseeb Ahmad for London Marathon. Sub 3 needs to be comfortable (entry sorted).

That tweet was posted by his most trusted guide, Duncan Shea-Simonds. Unfortunately Dunc couldn't guide him this time. So, Has' good friend Chris Sherwood would take him through the first half but they needed a second guide to complete the race – hopefully in a sub-three time.

I offered to help as I felt capable of completing the job, plus I had already arranged to go down to London to support a friend of mine who was doing it – in the event my friend didn't do it and ended up supporting us instead!

We met at the ExCel on the Friday to register and have a brief run. I immediately felt comfortable with Has and knew I'd made a good decision to help out – I think it would be fair to say we clicked.

This was the very first time I had met Rodge and his friend Mark. Just before my practice run with Rodge I had left all my stuff with Mark. I hadn't met either of these guys before. When we had finished our run, Mary and I walked back through the ExCel Centre. I asked her where my rucksack and coat were. She said she didn't know.

"Oh my God, I left them back there with Rodge's friend."

Mary had spotted what she perceived as 'dodgy'-looking people hanging around. My wallet and phone were in my jacket. I wasn't bothered about my wallet but my whole life is on that phone. We turned around and legged it back outside. Phew – Mark was there and said that Rodge had gone back in to look for me.

A sleepless night behind me, and with nerves jangling I travelled down to Blackheath, the start of the race, with Mary and met a couple of my friends at the station including Chris Sherwood, who was going to help with the first half of the marathon. I thought this would be helpful to Rodge as he could observe how Chris guided me and it would take some of the load off Rodge. It was a lot to ask of someone I had only met once, to take me through all 26.2 miles. Considering human traffic, bottles, narrow sections, twists and turns, speed bumps and supporting and encouraging me when I drop the pace, it's no mean feat.

We went towards the red pen and waited for Rodge to turn up. We waited and waited and he was nowhere to be seen. My heart really sunk; where was he? My other friend Martin Burder, who was in the blue start, asked to go into the red pen to help me out.

The marshal in charge wasn't having any of it. "No, he already has two guides." I just wasn't sure what to do.

When we got into the pen, who should pop up but Rodge!

"Hey, mate, where have you been? I was getting worried." A huge sense of relief swept over me. We literally had ten minutes to go before countdown and the excitement mounted. This was it: my stab at a sub-three marathon.

As we set off in the mass start, slightly downhill, I felt very nervous. Bodies and legs moved together in a swarm of human energy. Adrenaline laced everyone's veins and it would be so easy to overcook it at the start. Chris Sherwood was guiding me for the first half and we did a brisk 6.40 for the first mile. Too quick, I thought, however, we soon settled into a 6.50 minute per mile pace. As we progressed, weaving in and out of the slower runners, dodging bottles and trying to get fluid on board at each aid station, the miles ticked off. We got to halfway in 1.29. Bang on pace. But this was where Rodge was meant to take over and he was nowhere to be seen. Chris told me not to worry.

We got to mile fourteen and Rodge popped up. "Sorry, chaps, but I had to run back and get a gel as I was flagging."

Sounds a bit ominous, I thought, but anyway, he was here and he took over.

We kept the pacing bang on 6.50 for another six to eight miles. When we got to twenty-four miles I began to feel the pacing – and not only the pacing, but the physical toll of the high levels of concentration I have to conjure up in order to stay alert, listening to my guide giving me instructions in order to avoid collision and keep up. So, the last four miles were extremely tough.

My legs just wanted to stop turning and I felt them seizing up, but Rodge kept on shouting at me to carry on: "Come on, mate, think of your daughters, how proud they would be."

I would have laughed at him if I'd had the energy because I only have one daughter. I probably would have said, "Is there something you know that I don't?" Anyway, it worked and I just kept going and going. I had to dig pretty damn hard for the last mile but we were on target and there was no way I was going to stop now.

As we entered the finishing shoot and crossed the line Rodge shouted, "You did it, Has – 2.59.23!"

I instantly collapsed and was put on a stretcher. I felt so ill and I couldn't speak at all; I think the paramedics were genuinely worried. I knew I was fine, just completely exhausted. Once I managed to be sick I felt a great deal better and Rodge and I made our way to the Guide Dogs Association (GDA) reception area.

Rodge's reflections of race day are as follows:

We arranged where to meet up on the day as we had access to the very front of the red start. I eventually found Has and Chris about five minutes before the start – we clarified our tactics and set off on the gun. It was a gorgeous day and I was excited to be there.

Fast-forward to thirteen miles – Chris, having done a superb job, had got Has through in around one hour twenty-eight minutes, so he handed me the tether. All we had to do was keep going at that pace for another thirteen miles!

If you've ever run a marathon you'll understand, but until you're over the finish line nothing's guaranteed. We were both feeling it but we dug deep and hung on – eventually coming home in two hours, fifty-nine minutes and twenty-three seconds. He beat me by one second – that's how competitive he is!

I did have a few minutes of worry as Has had put that much in, he was stretchered off and taken to the medical tent.

I followed him there and his first words to me were, "We did it, buddy!" Amazing...

He did rope me into guiding him on another marathon – and the story's very similar!

Haseeb epitomises the attitude 'You can do anything if you put your mind to it.'

One of the most inspiring people I have ever met, and a good friend.

After the race Rodge and I hobbled gingerly over to the GDA reception area. This was reserved for family and athletes, and I met a friend I had lost touch with over twenty-five years previously. We had been reunited through Facebook a few months earlier and Mark Saunders, a very close school friend of mine, agreed to meet me after the race. It was so incredibly moving. We had so much to catch up on but it wasn't going to happen just yet as I wasn't in a state to have a coherent conversation.

Well, it was an awesome weekend. Reunited with my long-lost buddy and a sub-three marathon. A job well done.

I knew that having just smashed out the best marathon performance of my life, the season ahead looked extremely promising. The marathon training always gives me a great endurance base to work from. I was so looking forward to the triathlon season, which would start in May. What would this season bring? A shower of podium results was what I was hoping for, and a place on the World Class Programme for Rio.

CHAPTER 18

ROAD TO RIO BLOCKED

I took a well-earned rest after the London Marathon. Needless to say, it took a lot out of me. However, I knew it would set me up well for the rest of the season. Once recovered I would experience a reasonably successful 2014 triathlon season. Although, there were going to be a number of unexpected twists and turns to come.

Earlier in the year I had found out that the BTF had decided to match Chris Goodwin up with Ben Matthews, who had guided me in the previous year. I was gutted to say the least. It wasn't anyone's fault but I was naturally very disappointed. Finding good guides isn't easy at all, but as luck would have it a young triathlete by the name of Andrew Whiteley, who was studying at Loughborough University, had expressed an interest in guiding. I arranged to meet up with him during February and we went for a run. We hit it off straight away, literally! On our first run Andrew had misjudged how wide the path was and my right hand clipped a lamp post and made an almighty clang. Probably sounded worse than it was; it did hurt a little but not too badly. Andrew was mortified, however I got to really like him and he really reminded me of my youngest brother – always happy and constantly singing. Our very first race was the Leicester Triathlon, which went extremely well and set us up nicely for my first international race of the year in France later in the month.

The day after we arrived in Besançon, Andrew and I went for a swim following a very hearty breakfast. Yes, it was hearty indeed. Andrew looked after me good and proper. I'd ask for a small bowl of cereal and he would come back with a huge quantity of three different cereals mixed together. The man loves his cereal. The pool was awesome, fifty metres with razor-sharp lane ropes which my right arm seemed to like rubbing itself against, and I ended up with serious lane-rope rash. In fact my swim hat got caught up at one time and the lane rope ripped a hole in it, I'm not kidding.

A day before the race, Alastair Donaldson, one of the BTF officials who was assigned to manage the GB Squad, got an email informing him that all the visually impaired triathletes were to go through a classification process. We rocked up to the place where this was happening near the hotel. Once we got in I was asked a barrage of questions by the IPC-approved ophthalmologist classifier. After a number of questions and basic visual field tests I was classified as B1 (totally blind). This was the first year that the International Triathlon Union had introduced a factoring system to attempt to level the playing field. My category got three minutes and forty-three seconds' factoring. In other words, if you are totally blind you get a 3.43 head start in the race. This apparently is meant to level the playing field for the totally blind athletes.

The ITU had been undertaking some research into the time difference between the totally blind and partially sighted athletes across the three disciplines, even though the sample sizes would have been so small that the results would have been statistically unsound. As it happened, I was the only athlete who got the factoring. One of the previously B1 athletes from Germany got reclassified as a B2. Clearly this had major implications in respect of potential placing for those B1 athletes who were reasonably quick and the partially sighted guys who have the advantage of varying degrees of vision. The B1 athletes, however, had to wear blacked-out glasses on the run.

On the day of the race what I remember most is that the sun was beaming through our hotel room; it was a beautiful day. I switched on my Blue tooth speaker and played Spandau Ballet's Gold through it at high volume. This got me and Andrew in the right frame of mind for the race. Once we had made our way down to race registration and got all the usual checks out of the way, we walked up to the swim start. Unfortunately I didn't have my shoes with me and it was a painful walk on rough tarmac. When we eventually got there it was time to prepare for what was going to be the most incredible swim of my life. I've done river swims before, and swum in the sea, but never down a fast-flowing river. We had to swim up to a rope and hold on until the race hooter was sounded.

Everyone hung on to the rope and I could hear cries of, "Oh my God." All I can say is that it felt as though a giant hand was swinging the rope violently to shake us off. For me it was actually fine as I was tethered to Andrew and my legs were behind the rope. As soon as the hooter sounded, we were off. To me the swim just felt a little more frantic than normal and I kept a cool head, trying to keep form and swim as normally as possible. Not being able to see, I just have to feel the water and the body position of my guide next to me. I used the tension of the tether and Andrew's body position to gauge what I needed to do but there was no telling how well I was swimming, as sometimes I felt the catch and other times it felt quite choppy and disjointed.

The swim just happened so fast I couldn't believe it when we hit the shore. I kind of knew I would possibly get a personal best, but not a 750-metre swim in 7.16 – that was simply insane! Earlier in the season I had been swimming better than I had ever swum, achieving times of around 13.30 for a 750-metre swim. Anyway, this meant that I wasn't as exhausted as I might otherwise have been and we ran through transition as planned, and got straight onto the bike without incident. This was a technical bike course but we had ridden it at least three times in preparation so we knew what to do.

On the first lap, I heard a bang and a few minutes later Andrew told me that the Slovenian pair who were in front of us were out with a puncture. Into T2 and we were doing extremely well. I felt really good on the run. Andrew, who had worked really hard on the bike, was feeling it a little in the first 2k or so but found his form after that. We passed the Germans with two hundred metres to go, and then we crossed the finish line.

I was greeted by a very nice French marshal, who turned out to be my chaperone for my dope test. He congratulated me and said that I came fifth overall.

I said, "Fifth?" He confirmed this, and I asked, "Is that with the factoring?"

He replied, in his beautiful French accent, "I do not know – you came fifth overall." I knew that I had done well but was not sure of my actual positioning at this stage.

The dope test took what seemed like forever. I wasn't allowed a recovery drink and was only allowed to drink out of a water bottle they provided for me. A female official (who I found out later was the lead anti-doping official) was insisting that I go for my dope test in my tri-suit but fortunately Alastair made her see sense.

Once we got to the hotel where the dope test was taking place, the form-filling was painfully slow as her English wasn't great (understandably), but she didn't seem to understand that we needed to get back for the medal ceremony. Sadly we missed this due to the slowness of the officials involved and a lack of understanding of the rules. Really I should have had some recovery food and drink within twenty minutes of the race. It was almost an hour later when Alastair snuck me a banana.

All in all, this was another amazing adventure with a brilliant outcome. Andrew and I got the gold we worked so hard for. It was lovely to have a small team out in Besançon, guys I got to know better, and spend time with people I love and respect.

Andrew has captured his memories of our time together in his own words:

"All right, mate?!" I'm not quite sure what I was expecting, but it wasn't the chatty London accent coming at me through the phone. It was the first time I'd spoken to Has, my allocated athlete in the GB Paratriathlon Squad, and I hadn't the first idea what a profound impact he and the whole experience would make on my life – but don't tell him that, he gets enough praise as it is.

We arranged our first meeting at his place in Leicester, and when he opened the door with his hand outstretched, it suddenly occurred to me that he is blind. All the time. He's not just a blind athlete who has to swim, cycle and run without the privilege of sight, he has to work, cook, greet and navigate all the complexities and intricacies of life we all find tricky enough as it is.

He also has to train, and that's exactly what I was there to have a go at.

"It's just a modified dog lead," he said as I took the running tether, and after a few worryingly brief tips on guiding, we were off. After navigating the curbs, corners and crossings we arrived at a stretch of wide footpath alongside the A6. Things were going well, and I'd been quietly impressed with myself, fuelled by Has' characteristic encouragement, for how quickly I'd picked up the basics.

Well into a repetition of a two-minute-race pace effort, sailing spectacularly over the ground, our flow was halted by a loud metallic clang, immediately followed by a sharp tug on the tether. I spun round to see Has bent double, head in hands. I'd neglected to remember that we were now two people wide, and didn't give a lamp post a large enough berth.

"It's okay, I've had worse." Certainly, I had rarely felt worse.

Fortunately, Has is the gracious type, and after eleven races, four training weekends, two weeks away, many training days and a disproportionate number of nights in hotel rooms for two people not romantically involved with one another, I can honestly say that guiding is right up there among the best things I've done with my life.

I am, of course, very proud and a little bit smug that Has won an ITU World Series race with me at the other end of the tether.

The race suited him perfectly; a river swim with a current so strong people were being washed downstream after missing the exit ramp, and a run slightly longer than the usual five kilometres. The gun went, the swim was utter chaos and the bike was solid. Within the first five hundred metres of the run, he set a ferocious pace and I was struggling. This was not good; all sorts of things were on the line. So, cunningly, I did the decent thing. Stifling my heavy breathing as best I could, I asked Has in an almost condescending tone if he was sure he could keep this pace for the full five kilometres.

He tossed a casual "Yeeeah" over his shoulder to me. I began to wonder how effective navigating the route by trial and error would be for a blind man, should I need to let him run ahead.

Luckily for him, and for the spectators who'd rather not have a small, sweaty man careering into them, I soon found my feet and we glided across the line victorious. An incredible day and an amazing win for Has.

I mulled over how to end this little piece without it sounding like an obituary (although at least it'll save me a job when the time comes), so I'd like to end with a message to you, Has. Essentially, I just want to say thank you to a friend. The times we spent together, the things we achieved, the team we formed were truly the stuff of stories. Thanks for sharing with me and caring for me. Thanks for the little things: the embarrassment of you finding a spanner in an

*instant where I had failed after ten minutes of searching, the time
our conversation was so deep the three-hour drive to Slough felt
like twenty minutes, and the unique experience of sightseeing with
a blind man. And here's to more moments like those.*

*There are few people for whom I'd read aloud an entire Italian
menu in my best (worst) accent three times over – only for them to
choose lasagne. Has, you are one of them.*

A couple of weeks later I was guided by another one of my guides
I have got to know extremely well, Jack Peasgood. Another
very impressive young man who has superb guiding skills and
athleticism for racing, and such a phenomenal caring nature to
support his paratriathlete friends in and around events, Jack
has become one of my close friends, as have many of my guides
throughout the years.

The Hyde Park Race was part of the World Series and I was
looking forward to it on the back of my success in France. The
swim went as well as I could have hoped, in fact better than
expected. The previous year my 750-metre open-water time
was around fifteen minutes. I managed a 13.30 swim with Jack
– one and a half minutes quicker, a substantial improvement
thanks to Richard Chipps' swim coaching and my self-belief.
Many thought I wouldn't be able to improve, including some
people who were very close to me, but I never gave up. Here I
was coming out in a reasonably good time and putting myself in
contention for a top-five finish. Finishing in the top six meant
championship points and contributed to world ranking places.

So, Jack and I smashed out a stonking bike section, including
carving up a cone when going around a sharp corner as a result
of me getting out of my saddle too soon, something I did
coming out of dead turns in order to get up to speed. On the run
I was ahead of my GB compatriot Iain Dawson but my other GB
Team mates, Dave Ellis and Chris Goodwin, were too far ahead

to catch. Chris was at this time still a B1 classification and had the same factor of 4.3. I didn't realise until the end that I was in fourth position. A Slovenian pair were just ahead of me. I didn't really push too hard for the last 1k as I thought the third position I was in was safe. Unfortunately I finished in fourth position but this was okay; I was third GB in. Surely my European slot was in the bag?

The BTF, despite my excellent results, didn't invite me to go to the European Championships. I was very disappointed, and in fact I was angry. How could they do this to me after such great results? The other three GB Team members had secured their slots for the European Championships in Austria. So, to make myself feel better I did a little standard-distance race at Wicksteed Country Park, Kettering with my friend Kieron Ford, who is my strength and conditioning coach. It was a good distraction.

In July 2014 I flew to Iseo, Italy to do another ITU race with Andrew. Unfortunately, this race was a huge disappointment and as we set out, the conditions got very choppy. I didn't expect it at all and started to hyperventilate. I had to stop twice and Andrew was brilliant and told me to take my time to recover, but in my heart, I knew I had blown the chance to podium. The bike section went extremely well and we made at least one place back, and I smashed out the best run of the season. Yet, it wasn't enough and I finished seventh out of eight.

When we returned to the hotel I expected one of the coaches to at least say something empathetic but this didn't happen. Not one word of consolation was forthcoming. This made me feel even more despondent about my result. A few positive words of encouragement wouldn't have been misplaced.

I knew, following the disappointment of this race, that I wouldn't be invited to the World Championships in Canada in September. There were only two slots available for the GB males and I had a feeling that Chris Goodwin and Dave Ellis would get automatic places. I applied anyway and was told what I already knew. In Canada all the athletes who hadn't been previously classified went through a classification process. Chris Goodwin was reclassified as a B2 and his factoring was removed. Neither of the GB VI males podiumed. This was clearly not the result the GB Team were hoping for and I'm sure very disappointing for the athletes concerned.

The next race for me was in Madrid towards the middle of September. This was a fantastic opportunity to show everyone that Iseo was just a minor blip. I asked Carl Shaw to guide me. He is a well-known local Leicestershire triathlete who did a stint as Iain Dawson's guide. I knew Carl was a phenomenal athlete and I couldn't understand why Iain had dropped him as a guide the previous season. Well, his loss was my gain and Carl's brilliant attention to detail and hunger to win proved to be a real advantage. He even brought along his own race wheels to stick on the Matrix tandem we were going to race on. The tandem belonged to the BTF, who didn't have enough race wheels to go around. I had in the past ended up with training wheels, and maybe race wheels if I was lucky. Maybe one day I could afford to invest in my own Matrix tandem with top-notch wheels.

Everything just fell into place on race day. A little warm-up swim beforehand and we were ready to rock and roll. Out of the water in my quickest time for a 750-metre swim that season; the bike section was out of this world. We had the fastest bike split, and with the run left we were in second position. I was catching the Ukrainian B1 athlete, but unfortunately there wasn't enough of the run course left and I finished only forty seconds behind. If only there had been another five hundred metres left, but regardless, I was so happy.

I went to get a massage and it was so lovely that a number of the other GB Squad members came over to congratulate me. One of the coaches, the same guy out in Iseo earlier in the year who failed to lift me from my deep disappointment, came across and enthusiastically shook my hand and told me well done. It's funny how people react when you have done really well compared to the occasions when things aren't going so well. Now I always make a point of putting my arm around those who don't do as well as they would have liked. After all, life isn't all about winning and hitting those podium spots. It's also about what you learn on that journey of missed opportunities – mistakes as well as the successes.

After coming back from Madrid, I had already booked myself onto a standard-distance race in Eton Dorney Lake. I hadn't expected to go to Madrid, being a late entry, so Eton Dorney was a fun race with Andrew. It was a non-para triathlon race so I was racing against able-bodied guys.

My fastest standard distance prior to this race was around two hours and thirty-two minutes. When Andrew asked me what I hoped to do I told him what I thought he wanted to hear: "I think something like two hours and ten minutes."

"Yes, that's what I had in mind."

Actually I thought, *You're having a laugh, mate!* In the end we smashed out a two-hour-and-eight-minute standard-distance time and I won my age category. I honestly couldn't believe it. I kept giggling when we finished because I just didn't think I would smash over twenty minutes off my previous PB. A great end to a highly enjoyable season.

All that was left was to wait for the IPC announcement on which categories were going to be included in the 2016 Rio Paralympic Games. On the 7th October 2014, an announcement was made on the six out of ten categories across the paratriathlon sport which were going to be included and the VI males were not in.

Initially I took the news in my stride. I was contacted by

many friends who were very sympathetic. It wasn't really until a week later that it all hit home. I had a meeting with my swim coach Richard Chipps, who had told me that if I carried on with the World Class Programme he would be happy to continue coaching me. I had agreed to start paying him for this. If not, then Richard would move on to other interests, which was quite reasonable. He had been coaching me since 2008 and not asked for a penny. In return I had been paying for his travel and accommodation to international races. The coaching had now come to an end. I went to the pool the following week and swam without Richard Chipps coaching me. Absent was his instructions, guidance and constant encouragement. I felt such sadness in my heart. I felt quite alone, and to be honest a little lost. What would I do next, and what kind of support would I get if I did decide to continue in triathlon? I knew I would have to dig deep if I was to take the next tentative steps in rebuilding any triathlon plans.

CHAPTER 19

TIME FOR CHANGE

After the devastating news of non-inclusion in the Paralympics I had to refocus my energies towards something else that would help me to forget about what had just happened. I'm very good at removing negativity from my mind, setting new goals and targets and, dare I say it, running away from or avoiding things which are hurtful. So the hurt of not having the chance to get to Rio meant that one door had shut, but despite the cliché, I truly am a great believer in the idea that if one door shuts then another opens.

I began to look at the possibility of running in GB colours in the London Marathon IPC World Cup. I started to make enquiries to British Athletics and found out that my sub-three-hour marathon time earlier in 2014 would be good enough to qualify for the following year. However, I still had to apply to British Athletics for the slot, which I subsequently did. I found out in early January that my application was rejected on a technicality but there was still a chance that I might get an invitational spot. A few weeks later the great news came through that I had got in. In the meantime I had fabulous friends who were lobbying the likes of Tanni Grey-Thompson and Lord Sebastian Coe. The only issue remaining was classification. My ITU classification wasn't going to be good enough because I was only classified by one classifier and the IPC rules are that there should be two present in any process, but that was okay because I could get classified in London prior to the race.

Everything was set. I had knocked out a 1.23 half-marathon in December 2014 at the Turkey Trot Race in Nottinghamshire, incidentally my fastest half-marathon to date. Training was going so well and I was on good form. My coach, Claire Shea-Simonds, had upped the thresholds of my training, targeting a 2.50 marathon. This was looking increasingly likely as I was hitting the targets she set me for each session. It was a tough regime though, and I was beginning to become fatigued towards February. Would I break, I wondered?

In the middle of February 2015 I came down with a virus. After I started to recover I decided to pop down to the gym for a light run. My daughter, a burgeoning talent where running was concerned, was on the treadmill next to me and as I increased the speed I felt a bit of discomfort in my right foot. As I brought the speed up to around twelve kilometres per hour (my easy-paced running speed), I experienced a sharp pain in the side of my foot so I hastily stopped the treadmill and stepped off; could it be cramp? I tried to massage it off but it was no good. I could hardly walk on it and my daughter helped me out of the gym.

I feared that it could be a stress fracture so popped down to the hospital a few days later, but nothing showed on the X-ray. With only a couple of months to go this couldn't have happened at a worse time. Just to rule out a stress fracture I decided to pay for an MRI scan. At this point I still had hope and tried to remain positive. The results came back and it was bad news. The results showed a stress fracture of the third metatarsal. I was told by the fracture clinic at Leicester Royal Infirmary that there would be twelve weeks where I couldn't run. I had been sent GB kit by British Athletics, and it was a cool Nike kit that I was looking forward to wearing. When I informed the governing body of the bad news they sent me a very nice email stating that they were very sorry that I couldn't compete but could I please send back the kit they had posted to me.

I was devastated. It was a massive blow once again but there was nothing that I could do. The priority had to be to get healthy. I had so many positive messages from close friends including Dunc, who messaged me saying that *You can't keep a good man down. You'll come back stronger, buddy*, which meant the world to me.

The following few months were all about painstaking rehabilitation. Hours and hours spent in the pool aqua-jogging. For anyone who wants to know what this is, it basically consists of a float which you tie around your midriff that enables you to jog along in the pool.

When I explain what aqua-jogging is to non-athletes the response I get is, "That sounds like fun!" Let me assure you, it definitely isn't fun. I would sometimes spend two hours jogging in the pool trying to keep my run fitness up. It was so incredibly boring. However, I was lucky as there were a number of great lifeguards, like a young man by the name of Ki Hepworth who chatted to me as I jogged along. I also invested in a SwiMP3 player – anything to kill the boredom, but if this was what it took to get me back to fitness so it would be less of a slog when I got back to actual running, then this was what I was going to do. It was all about the long game. I had the bigger picture in mind but I just wasn't sure what I was going to do next. I needed a challenge, some kind of goal. I certainly am not the kind of guy who can just hang back and wait for things to happen to me. Life is too short for all that.

So, I had a little think. I had always wanted to do a half-Ironman. Many of my friends had completed the Vitruvian Race at Rutland Water in recent years. This consisted of a 1,900-metre swim, a fifty-two-mile bike ride and then a 13.1-mile run. I heard that the run was nice and flat so I wasted no time and registered for the race, which was towards the end of August.

In the meantime, my running was starting to come back but there was still some pain. How long was it going to take, I kept asking myself? Everything I was reading and all the advice I was getting was that the pain I was experiencing was adaptive discomfort as the bones remoulded. I could tell that my biomechanics had also been affected. This was going to be a long process, but I had time as the Vitruvian wasn't until the 21st August. Slowly but surely my runs got longer and longer, starting from fifteen minutes and increasing in 10% increments every week, and things were beginning to look promising by the end of July.

The Vitruvian Race was something I was really looking forward to but there was definitely a tinge of trepidation. The longest races I had done were standard-distance triathlons (1,500 metres swim, 40k bike and 10k run). The Vitruvian was 1.2 miles swimming, fifty-two miles on the bike and a half-marathon (13.1 miles) run. Training had been going well and my tapering (reducing the volume of training a week or two before the race) had been carefully planned by my coach. In fact for many people the taper is a difficult period of training. This is when the mind starts to play games with you. The body and brain realise that you are reducing the level of training and muscles start to seize up. For me, I start to feel lethargic and niggles I thought I didn't have start to surface. However, I really did feel like I was coming down with a virus a couple of days before the race.

On the morning of the Vitruvian Race Andrew Whitely, my guide, came to pick me up in his amazing camper van. There was plenty of room for my tandem in the converted Ford Transit, and Andrew loved his four-wheeled mobile home.

As we loaded the van at 5.30 in the morning, my next-door neighbour stuck her head out of the window and shouted, "Can you please keep the noise down?!" Oops! We obviously weren't being very considerate in our early-morning movements.

Once we got to the venue I noticed that the early-morning start and the effects of tapering left me more than a little tired. I was convinced that I was coming down with something. The side of my tongue was sore, a tell-tale sign in my case that something was up. We were greeted by Andrew's mum and dad, which took my mind off the race for a short while, and the sun started to rise – it was going to be a beautiful day.

We got into our wetsuits, ready for my first middle-distance triathlon. The swim involved two laps, and after the first lap getting out and running for a short distance onshore before jumping back in; a little awkward for Andrew and me to manoeuvre but nonetheless the swim went very well with a sub-forty-minute 1,900 metres.

I knew we would be strong on the bike but it was back to my old sports tandem and I knew it wouldn't have the same level of performance as the Matrix race tandem. Still, a 2.25 bike section wasn't too shoddy and was done without too much fatigue. Coming off the bike I desperately needed the loo and so did Andrew. Many triathletes on the longer-distance bike sections actually pee on the bike but I couldn't bring myself to do that, so Andrew guided me to the Portaloo. Little did I know that this was the only toilet in transition and Andrew was waiting outside for his turn. This probably took three or four minutes off my overall time.

No matter, loo break done, it was on to the run. After the initial stiffness of coming off the bike I felt myself getting stronger and stronger on the run, and I could sense us overtaking people as Andrew gave me each mile split as we smashed out mile after mile. It was lovely hearing the crowd cheer us on, and the familiar voices of friends and family cheering us on in the background were uplifting. The last couple of miles were very challenging as I developed a stitch in the last kilometre; obviously I took on too much fluid or gel, or both, on the run. However, I smashed out a 1.32-hour run split, which was amazing. My overall time was four hours and forty-three minutes. Wow, I really didn't expect to go that much under five hours, and if it wasn't for the toilet break we probably would have been nearer the 4.30 mark.

All of Andrew's family were there and there was plenty of support from friends along the course. It was an incredible race and I loved every minute of it. Andrew's family were absolutely lovely and to top it all I met little Parker, Andrew's brother's Labrador puppy; a real cutie.

Following the Vitruvian, I did come down with a heavy cold, so I wasn't just imagining my symptoms (for a change) in the run-up to the event. I have no idea if it affected my overall performance. Probably not. Thankfully, this was effectively the last triathlon race of the season. When I get to the end of the season I have to admit I really need a break from training and all the planning which goes into the logistics of getting to races.

I had, however, one more endurance event left: another crack at a fast marathon. I had entered the Leicester Marathon taking place in mid October. I originally had asked a friend, Dan Leak, a lovely guy I had hooked up with through Guiderunning. UK, to guide me Unfortunately Dan was injured so I drafted in Rodge Wilkins to help me out. He saved my bacon once more.

On the day of the marathon I wasn't fully recovered from the Vitruvian. My right hip and back were very tight and I knew once we got to halfway and the clock was on 1.30 that I wouldn't go under three hours. It was also becoming evident that the course was going to be more technical than I thought. One section was practically running down an alleyway in single file. Rodge told me to run in front of him as he tried valiantly to steer me through. As we reached fourteen miles and headed out into the countryside, there were sections where we had to go onto pavements and step off. This constant stepping on and off took a lot of concentration and effort. It was physically and mentally demanding.

At one point I said to Rodge, "Is the road coned off because we sound like we are very near the traffic?"

Rodge told me later that he didn't want to worry me, so answered, "Just keep to that line, Has, and you'll be fine." In actual fact I was on the road and Rodge took the grass verge but the road hadn't been closed for the race. The lack of fitness, technical sections and a hard season meant a 3.9 marathon finish and another visit to the medical tent.

After the Leicester Marathon I decided to give paracycling a go and Andrew and I entered the National Time Trial Race in Derby. This was a ten-mile time trial with hand cycles and tandems racing one another for the national crown. When it came to our turn we blasted off as fast as we dared. As it was on main roads we had to be mindful of the traffic and comply with the Highway Code. When we finished we thought we had come third. However, when the trophies were given out it was evident that we came fourth, the reason being that the female tandem pairs were factored. So, although we did actually come third the women in fourth place had the factor, which bumped up their position to third. Iain Dawson was also racing but unfortunately he suffered yet another puncture. The guy had his third or fourth puncture of the season; such bad luck. He seemed to take it in his stride.

Over the winter I considered what races to do in 2016. I had been thinking of doing an Ironman, albeit fleetingly. The idea first arose in a little bit of banter between my coach's husband, Dunc, and myself.

"I'd love to guide you in your first Ironman, dude." He then tweeted on a few occasions to his Ironman buddies that *Has is thinking of doing an Ironman*. I was never really that serious about it to tell you the truth. I couldn't think of anything worse than doing hours and hours of racing, from early morning to early evening. I mean, what crazy types would put themselves through that amount of pain and suffering?

Still, with all the events of the recent past the prospect of completing an Ironman began to seem rather attractive. I would be guided by a friend who not only wanted to do it, but had a considerable pedigree in completing sub-eleven Ironman races. Dunc has not only completed run-of-the-mill Ironman races (if you could ever call them that), but some extreme races such as Norseman, an Ironman race which takes you up a mountain! So, after discussion with Dunc, I registered for the Barcelona Ironman race. When I looked at the date of the race, it was the 2nd October, the same date as my daughter's birthday. *A great omen*, I thought, *this is meant to be.*

I also signed up to a couple of half-Ironman races to ensure that I got plenty of racing in before the big day. However, in October 2015 when I signed up to all of these races, the 2nd October 2016 seemed such a long time away. There was so much training to be done in the run-up to it and a lot of it had to be done by myself. The hardest parts of this would be the swimming – with no swim coach and improvements to be had, I wasn't sure I could do it but with no choice I just soldiered on.

The New Year did bring some good news. Claire, my coach, was now working for the local triathlon haunt Race Hub, and Jonny Nicol, the manager, generously took me on as a member of the Racetime Team. I was chuffed to bits. I hadn't been part of any team apart from the GB Squad. This would definitely help with new equipment such as running shoes, wetsuit, tri-suit and kitbags, and general support. It really gave me a lift, which I so desperately needed. Training can be a lonely business at the best of times but knowing you are part of a team is psychologically beneficial.

So then it was a question of focusing on the early part of the season, which for me is always dominated by road racing. It was time to have some fun. Claire had built in a lot of cross-training involving more biking and swimming. The difference with the training this season was going to be the brick sessions on a Wednesday. A brick session is when you do a run straight after riding the bike. My sessions were in the gym where they had Wattbikes, and my training sets were very specific so I needed gym staff to help me out. A young guy called Dan Chapman had been trained on the Wattbike and he was very bright and understood that I needed some support with getting statistical feedback. So, he stood next to me and gave me the feedback I needed. Not only that, but he encouraged me to push harder. He didn't have to do that, but he did and for that I am truly grateful. There are other guys in the gym, Aman Singh and James, who have also provided me with support and encouragement. You guys are awesome.

I had entered the London Marathon, taking place in April, as a 'good for age' entrant. Tim Heming, with whom I had done some training a couple of years previously, agreed to guide me for London and two half-marathons in the run-up to it. My aim for London was to go under three hours once more. I wasn't sure this was possible in all honesty as I know that getting over a stress fracture can take more than twelve months. However, I'm not one to shy away from ambitious goals; the gauntlet had been laid down.

I decided to do the Cambridge Half-Marathon in February 2016, one of the reasons being that my daughter was studying at Anglia Ruskin University and she was able to register me for the race. She had also registered, and I think this was the first race we were doing together. I met Tim on the morning of the race. I had considerable back problems in the run-up and hadn't trained for three days previously, constantly stretching and foam-rolling – I was not in a good way. However, I had ensured that I got up early and warmed my muscles up and once Tim and I had limbered up we got to the first pen feeling relatively confident. This was the first race I ever did with Tim, so it was a whole new experience for him and he was absolutely fantastic. I started to flag towards the end of the race but he ensured that I got plenty of feedback on the beauty of the old city, pointing out various landmarks and points of interest, even though I wasn't in any fit state to take it in at the time. We crossed the line in one hour and twenty-five minutes. That was the target time I had been set by my coach, but it seemed harder than it should have been, probably because of my poorly back.

We went to take on some nutrition. I was expecting to see my daughter at around two hours. However, suddenly Tim shouted, "There's Ayeisha!" I thought, *That can't be right*, but there she was clocking in at around one hour and forty-eight minutes on very little training prior to the race.

"Daddy, Daddy, I didn't listen to a word you said and went out hard and hung on!" I had advised her to pace herself evenly over the 13.1 miles. Well, good on her – I was so proud of my little girl.

I thought nothing more of the Cambridge Half other than that it had been a positive experience for me, Tim, and of course my daughter. I went back to Leicester and planned my next race. Tim had suggested that we do Reading Half as preparation for London. I thought it a great idea and registered straight away. The race was on the 1st April and Mary and I booked our hotel room, making the two-hour journey the day before.

It was a beautiful morning on the day of the race and I felt a lot more rested and up for the challenge. Tim met us at the Madejski Stadium with his parents and daughter Laura; it was lovely to see him with his family, all of whom were so friendly and glad to be supporting us. Tim and I got ourselves ready for our second major race of the season. We got to the front and had plenty of space despite the fact that there were several thousand registered for the race.

There were some pretty fast guys out there. I turned to one of the other competitors and asked what he hoped to do.

"Oh, around sixty-seven minutes." Gulp.

This was a good race to do if you are blind as there was lots of space and relatively very few speed bumps and twists and turns. The crowd support was phenomenal and as we hit the five-mile mark there was a superb downhill section. I got carried away and ran full-speed down the hill. Oh, how I love a good downhill, and we easily went under a 5.30-minute mile. It felt so good; however I was to pay for this misdemeanour later: it was definitely a bad pacing decision on my part. A woman spectating at one part of the course tried to give me a drink and Tim had to point out to her that I couldn't see – the penny dropped and so did the bottle!

We finished with a time of 1.25.47. Slower than Cambridge but still a good result. But I knew I wasn't in the same shape I had been in during 2014 and the beginning of 2015. We went back to the hotel room where Tim and I showered (separately). When we were getting dressed Tim shared something with me which will never leave me and which completely floored me, in the sense that I had no idea what my good friend had been going through over the past year or so, and given this, had still come out and raced with me.

"Has, I don't know how to tell you this but we are such good friends and I want to share this with you. After the Cambridge Half-Marathon I got in the car to drive back home. I had to stop because I was in pieces. I stopped and broke down in floods of tears." Tim told me that he had been suffering with clinical depression. Getting out of bed was a struggle, let alone working up the motivation to run. I just felt so awful that he was going through this. But the incredible thing was, the only thing that kept Tim going was the fact that he didn't want to let me down.

I felt so humbled that this brilliant journalist by profession, a highly intelligent human being and talented runner, had developed a strong bond of friendship with me of all people.

Why me? The answer, I think, lies in the inextricable connection that develops between people who experience adversity. We both knew that feeling of darkness. Mine was a combination of losing my sight and having to rebuild my life. For Tim it was the blackness of deep depression, which only he can explain, and he does in some of his excellent blogs. I often think of Tim and some of my other friends who suffer from this illness, and when I do, I text them or drop them a line to just let them know that I am thinking of them and I care. That's all it takes sometimes. It's the least I can do. The London Marathon would bring Tim and me even closer as lifelong friends, beyond running or any other sport.

So, the London Marathon loomed closer. Only three weeks to go and the nerves started to kick in. Although Tim was guiding me he persuaded me to register someone who I had never met before, Ross Welton, as my main guide. I thought it best to do this as it's useful to have a second guide. However, I had done so much earlier in the season before I knew of Tim's mental health. Tim wanted to make sure that I had a guide just in case he wasn't able to guide me.

However, come race day both Tim and Ross ran either side of me. Over forty thousand people were registered. Even though I got a good-for-age start, it was packed. Ross did a great job as my 'domestique', carrying my gels and very politely removing other slower runners from my path!

A couple of times runners in front would exclaim, "Okay, mate, I know you're keen but take it easy." They would then turn their heads and realise there was a blind runner behind and start apologising profusely, ha-ha! At one stage Ross, in his keenness to help, actually tripped over my leg and went flying. Somehow he bounced on the floor and got back up and seemed right as rain.

Around eighteen miles I heard a loud bang and then all the

runners around me exclaimed, "Oooooh!" I asked Tim what had happened. Apparently a runner tried to run around some slower guys and ran slightly off course. He didn't notice a bollard and smacked straight into it. Race over for him. Ouch!

I knew in my heart that I wasn't going to go under three hours. I knew this at the halfway point, not because of the time – we had knocked out a 1.29 split – but more because of how I was feeling. In fact we were pretty much on target until around twenty-five miles where the wheels fell off. Tim just told me to relax and enjoy the rest of the race. So, I relaxed a bit and we crossed the finishing line with our hands joined.

After a short pit stop at the medical tent (where else?), we all made our way to the PDSA friends and family reception and I went for a massage. After some food, photographs and a natter I was told that Tim wasn't feeling very well. I was very worried about him but had to make my way back to my brother's house for dinner and get ready for our journey back home the following day. I heard that Tim was in a bad way afterwards with his stomach and mental fatigue. However, he did drop me a line to say he was okay a few days later, and that he was enjoying getting fat and drinking beer.

My final marathon time was 3.1.58, highly respectable and my second fastest marathon to date. Good enough for a 2017 good-for-age entry and another sub-three attempt.

It was time for a little break from training following London. I took two weeks off to recover and then the Ironman training would start in earnest. How would I cope with the increase in volume of training? Would I break and get injured? What support would I get to train? All these questions would be soon answered in time.

CHAPTER 20

LET'S HAVE A GO AT A WORLD RECORD

I took a well-earned rest after the London Marathon before embarking upon my Ironman training. Although it seemed daunting, the training wasn't so bad as my coach, Claire, eased me into it very gently. My training consisted of training six days a week with double sessions on some days. The brick sessions (Wattbike followed immediately by a run on the treadmill) were something I was familiar with but I hadn't done these sessions on a regular, week-in-week-out basis before. These sessions didn't start off particularly hard, but as the weeks wore on the sessions got tougher. The very intense sessions involved having to hold 160 watts average over ninety minutes followed by a forty-minute run at an average pace of fifteen kilometres per hour. The problem for me was firstly the heat in the gym – despite the fact that the air conditioning was switched on, it was still too warm for the session I was doing. I would sweat buckets on the Wattbike and then do the treadmill session already soaked through. I could hear my trainers squelching underneath me as I tried not to slip in the puddle of my own sweat. Yuck.

The other challenge I had was getting a member of gym staff to inform me, at regular intervals, that I was bashing out the thresholds set by my coach. I need not have worried as I was so lucky to have some awesome Everyone Active gym staff, such as Dan Chapman and Aman Singh, who practically stood next to me for more or less all of my sessions.

It does frustrate me that gym equipment isn't designed to be helpful to blind people who wish to operate the machines independently. This is something I would like manufacturers to be aware of and address in the future. It really can't be that hard in this day and age. On occasions I use my iPhone, which has voiceover built in that provides audible speech and works extremely well with the Stopwatch app. However, it can't tell me the speed or distance at which I am travelling. If I am on the tandem or out for a run with a friend I can now use Strava, another app which records speed, distance and maps the route you have taken. Technology has advanced so much that it has meant slightly less reliance on someone else telling me my training data.

During 2016 I still hadn't employed a swim coach. I no longer had support to get to Leicester Tri Club's Thursday-evening swims, which were at least thirty minutes' drive from my house. I carried on working in the pool by myself, knocking out intervals without knowing if my technique was correct or what times I was doing. The swim training is definitely the most challenging of the three disciplines of triathlon for me, much more so than running or biking. The thing which has always kept me going is the belief that I could still improve, or at least maintain my stroke from when I used to get coaching. So, I kept the faith and kept plugging away. Call it blind faith.

During the summer of 2016 I had two half-Ironman races booked before Ironman Barcelona and the National Paratriathlon Championships. The first was in Warwickshire, called The Avenger, and took place on the 12th June 2016. I had no idea what the course was like and I was told initially that the run course was off-road but manageable. With no other races in sight and this being the only one that Dunc could guide me in, I decided to register.

We picked a great day for the race. It was a glorious summer morning when we arrived at Ragley Hall, where the race started from. We rocked up to the lake, which was, we were told, a toasty seventeen degrees. However, I still wanted to get in and get warmed up.

As we got to the swim start Dunc asked me if I had the tether.

"No, mate, you had it last."

"Oh no, I left it in transition," Dunc replied. "Don't go anywhere, mate – I'll pop back and get it!" This isn't the first, nor will it be the last time when tethers have gone missing because the guide thinks I have it and I think the guide is in possession of the tether.

So, while I waited for Dunc to retrieve the tether, Claire Shea-Simonds was supporting and helped calm my nerves as all I wanted to do was get in the water and get started. Dunc soon came running back with the tether, much to my relief. Well, that was his warm-up sorted, now for my turn. Fortunately, there were a couple of minutes to turn the arms over before the starting hooter was sounded.

The swim was three loops of the lake. As we completed the second loop I started to tire. I really wondered how I was going to cope with the full Ironman swim, which was 2.4 miles as opposed to 1.2 miles for the half. By the time we had completed two and a half laps I was wishing for the swim to be over, and at last, we got to the exit and Dunc turned to me and told me the swim split. We had just done forty-five minutes. I was very disappointed, as I had previously knocked out thirty-nine minutes for a 1,900-metre swim. However, it wasn't all that bad – I found out later that the swim was 2,100 metres, two hundred metres longer than it was meant to be.

We were soon on the bike. I was feeling rather uncomfortable on the saddle after only twenty minutes on the tandem. I couldn't understand it, but thought maybe it was the new positioning on my brand-new Matrix. I had only just had a bike fitting a few weeks previously and perhaps some further adjustments were required. Later I found out that the seat post clamp was faulty and the saddle had tilted back. No wonder my undercarriage was so unforgiving.

Three quarters of the way through the bike section and we got a puncture. Dunc quickly changed the tyre, which had been glued on previously. He threw me the punctured tyre and told me to roll it up. I had no idea what I was doing and didn't do a great job. Dunc told me to chuck it. Shame – that was £75's worth of tyre which could have been repaired and reused. Oh well, with the puncture and the fact that we now had to take it a little more cautiously, we completed the bike section in 2.37 hours.

The run, however, was going to be four laps of challenging cross-country terrain with some small sections of tarmac. There was also a wooded section, which I think the organisers had purposefully placed there to provide Dunc and me with something extra to think about. This bit consisted of rutted tractor track with mud and demonic stinging nettles.

We aptly named this area the 'woods of peril'. "Here they come, Has, the woods of peril." Despite this I surprisingly smashed out a 1.40-hour split on the run and the overall time was pretty respectable all things considered: 5.09 hours.

I so love the post-race ambience. It's so relaxing after a race – all the tension is gone and I can focus on my second passion: talking to and meeting new people. I met Claire's cousin, Hayley and her (Hayley's) children, and another friend of theirs, Ollie Hatton, who I have since trained with, and we went for some teriyaki. I'd never eaten teriyaki before and didn't realise that the outside part is edible! Eating is always a challenge when you can't see and so I battled with a plastic fork, trying not to make a mess, when in actual fact I could have just picked it up with my hands and tucked right in. I so prefer finger food for that reason. That's why Indian cuisine is so much more accessible. It tastes great and you can eat it with your hands with impunity.

Earlier in the season I had decided to stick in a little sprint race and entered the National Paratri Championships in Liverpool, which took place a week prior to my next half-Ironman. I came second in the race with Carl Shaw as my guide. I felt so fatigued throughout the race, having done a heavy week of Ironman training (and I don't think the four hours of standing around the day before on a Zone 3 stall helped either – you live and you learn!). The swim was slow but we knocked out the fastest bike split of the day and I managed to trip on the run, again. The fall was a funny one really; a little dip, which you wouldn't notice ordinarily, but my foot found it and I sort of fell forwards and bounced on my belly a little. I was okay though and got up and carried on running. I was happy with the result: another silver medal bagged at the National Championships, and maybe this would help me to get back on the GB Squad for 2017.

A week later and I did the Cotswolds Classic with Kieron Ford guiding me. Kieron, my personal trainer, is someone who has helped me considerably over the past few years. He helped me out at a training camp in Majorca in 2014 a week before I smashed out my first sub-three-hour marathon. What an adventure the training camp was, particularly the near-death experience we had descending a mountain when the front tyre blew on our hire tandem. I felt the tandem tilt at an unusual angle and thought to myself, *That's odd*. The next second we careered into a ditch. Lucky for us it was a soft landing and we were both unscathed. Kieron was shaken but not stirred as it didn't put him off guiding me again.

The night before the Cotswolds Classic Race we stayed in a very posh B&B. Kieron said that it was a very romantic little place; the sort of place you would take your girlfriend or wife to. I noticed, as I was fumbling around getting used to my surroundings that in the bathroom there was a candleholder with a large candle right next to the toilet. I'd better watch out for that if I needed to go – it could be life-changing if I got it wrong. The landlord was a very posh dude who just wouldn't stop talking as soon as we walked through the door. He quickly started telling us of his chequered past. He apparently played the drums in Joe Cocker's band in the 1970s, until he decided to get himself a proper job, much to the relief of his father, a senior-ranking officer in the Merchant Navy.

It was yet another early-morning start, having to get up at 3.30am. This was truly horrible and is absolutely the worst thing about racing. The swim went well, even though Kieron told me later that for some reason we kept drifting to the right. He blamed my stroke, and I blamed his sighting! On the bike section we were doing so well but had to stop so that Kieron could help a woman who had come off her bike on one of the sharp corners. These things happen and it was absolutely the right thing to do.

The run course was even more difficult than The Avenger's. The single-track rutted terrain was arduous and hard going. It certainly slowed down our progress, which is incredibly frustrating for me. There were athletes overtaking me that I know on a much better course I would be well in front of. On one part of the multiple-lap course, there was a telegraph pole to jump over. We literally had to stop in front of it for me to negotiate it. There were probably only a thousand metres of tarmac where I was able to run freely and pick up my speed. This is when Kieron started to suffer, and he was very glad when we reached the single track once more.

On the last lap Kieron said, "Hold out your hand." I immediately held out my hand and felt a soft touch against it. "You just high-fived a kiddie." Cool. That was excellent hand-to-eye coordination on the part of Kieron, even though it was my hand and his eye!

Following the race, I did pick up a little niggle in my left foot, which was very worrying. I laid off training for a week and it settled down but didn't completely recover. I was very glad that I didn't have long left until Barcelona, but certainly the left foot was a worry.

My focus was now on being as fit and ready for the Barcelona Ironman as I could be. Dunc and I had bantered about doing an Ironman one day but I wasn't serious about it at all. Yet, once the decision had been made not to include my category in the Rio Paralympics, I felt I needed a big challenge to take my mind off what had happened. But I wasn't satisfied with just doing an Ironman. I decided to look up what the fastest blind Ironman record was. It currently stood at eleven hours, ten minutes and twenty-eight seconds. So there it was, ready for the taking. Again not satisfied with just breaking the world record, I wanted to ensure it was going to be official. So, I decided to apply to the *Guinness Book of Records* to see whether they would accept my application. I applied in June and a couple of months later I got a positive response, but they stipulated it had to be done blindfold. *Okay*, I thought, *how hard can that be? I can't see anyway, so wearing a blindfold shouldn't cause any problems other than discomfort.* And of course, it would have to be blacked-out goggles because of needing to wear them during the swim.

I asked my very good friends Martin and Joanna Westall to come to Barcelona with us in order that my family and I had support. With only a couple of weeks to go before we flew out, I also asked Martin to coordinate the evidence for the *Guinness Book of Records*. His help would prove invaluable. It took off the pressure of worrying about liaising with officials and allowed Dunc and me to concentrate on the logistics of racing.

We arrived at Calella on Friday 30th September and there was no time to waste. The climate was lovely, with the evening heat at a comfortable twenty-three degrees. As soon as we got to the hotel thirty minutes after leaving the airport (around 6.30pm), Martin and I made our way to registration. We met Dunc and went into the tent to register. It was oh so exciting.

Once registered Martin found the chief technical official. She would be instrumental in securing fifty-three handwritten statements from all the technical officials and marshals saying that they saw me wearing blacked-out goggles throughout the race. Of course there was the language barrier to contend with as Martin explained what we needed, but fortunately the combination of his ability to use sign language and the Spanish official's grasp of basic English worked a treat. With all of that sorted, we headed back to get ready for dinner at a local tapas restaurant, which had a *Star Wars* theme.

The following day Dunc and I went for a practice swim at 8am while the rest of the family went into Barcelona to do a bit of sightseeing. I could hear that the sea was a little choppy but Dunc reassured me that once we got through the worst of the waves (around 400 metres) heading out into the sea, and then a 90 degree right turn to swim parallel to the shore, the longest stretch of the course (around 1.9 kilometres), the sea would be far more calm. After the longest part of the swim was complete we would then do a 180 degree turn around the buoy to swim the remaining section, the fastest bit of the swim because of the way in which the water current worked. On the day of the race, Dunc explained, I would only feel a rolling sensation. Unfortunately when we started our swim practice I began to get anxious and my breathing went to pot. I had to stop and check my breathing, and when we did stop I felt the movement of the water as it tossed me around as if I was in a washing machine, and I started to feel sick. If you can imagine going into the sea when it is wavy and just shutting your eyes for five seconds, it is very frightening. At this point what was going through my mind was that I honestly didn't think that I was going to be able to even start the swim on the following day. My heart sank and I just felt so low.

Yes, I felt so despondent. How ridiculous, I had come all this way and completed all the training and the thought of not even being able to finish the swim made me feel very down indeed. There was no other option but to swim back to shore and start again. So I asked Dunc to take me back into the sea. The second time of asking I was able to get in and start swimming very comfortably. Thank goodness for that, but I still had that nagging feeling and worry in the back of my mind about what conditions to expect the following morning.

Dunc's mum, Janet, was onshore and was very supportive. "Now, Haseeb, don't you worry about swimming too fast, just take your time and do your own race. Don't worry about anyone else." In the meantime (as I found out later) Dunc was standing behind her rolling his eyes – as far as he was concerned, we were here to get around the course as fast as possible.

That afternoon, we racked the tandem. We were provided with racking space for at least ten bikes so we racked the tandem along the racking rail. It certainly got plenty of attention, with pictures of it being posted on the Barcelona Facebook page. We also organised our kit into individual bags we were provided with during registration. I normally have my kit laid out in transition, so this was a wholly new experience for me.

Once done with our pre-race preparations it was time to go back to the hotel and get something to eat. After dinner, my daughter popped into our apartment. I was busy packing my stuff for the race, a few final bits and bobs, when I overheard

Ayeisha telling her mum that she wasn't happy on her university course and she wanted to transfer. She was so upset, so I sat down with her and gave her a big cuddle and we talked things through. She said that she was sorry to land this on me the night before the race. I told her not to worry, after all it was only a race and not as important as her. This was absolutely the case, but something else which was going to play on my mind when trying to get to sleep that night.

CHAPTER 21

SUFFER LIKE A DOG

On the eve of the race there was a sudden and heavy downpour of rain, and consequently on the morning of the race (2nd October 2016) there was hardly any wind and the sea was as calm as a millpond. I walked down to Dunc's apartment with Martin. It was so quiet and tranquil. I knew it wasn't going to last long but the peace was very welcome right now as I gathered my thoughts. Once we joined Dunc and made our way down to the race start I couldn't hear the sea crashing onto the beach at all. I felt so happy and at ease. It was soon time to put on our wetsuits. It was so hot. My only regret was not taking a bottle of water down to where we queued up in our respective swim pens.

Dunc and I placed ourselves in the one hour and forty minutes pen for the rolling swim start. This was the sort of time my coach felt I could pull off. Moreover, we didn't want to get tangled up with the faster swimmers, which could have been counterproductive with people trying to swim in between us. There was a slight delay to the start as there was a power cut and the inflatable starting arch, which all the competitors were expected to pass under before entering the water, sagged sadly. Electricity was soon restored, and we were edging slowly towards it before the swim entry.

It was all very exciting, the hairs almost stood up on the back of my neck but the swim hat kept them in place. Everyone was chatting and in high spirits. I noticed that I was getting a little thirsty as the heat of the sun beat down on us. The decision not to bring a bottle of water with me was a regrettable one. As we got closer, the MC, Paul Kaye, gave Dunc and me a great shout-out and told everyone of our world record attempt. We got a wonderful cheer from the spectators and fellow competitors. It was a heart-warming moment.

The world record attempt was to go under the 11.10.28 set by Eric Manser in 2015 at the Florida Ironman. This was an unofficial world record, and Eric explains in his blog that he uses whatever useful sight he has to follow his guide. I can't say I blame him; wearing the blacked-out goggles (which was one of the conditions for the *GBR* world record attempt) made no difference to me apart from them being uncomfortable to wear for a long-distance race. The *Guinness Book of Records* insisted that the world record title had to be *The world's fastest Ironman blindfolded*. The reason for this is that the *GBR* rules stipulate that anyone should be able to have a crack at breaking the record, irrespective of background or ability. Someone who is sighted could have a go at the record, as long as they wear a blindfold. Yet, I couldn't attempt the world record sighted if I fancied it! However, I knew that blacked-out goggles or not, the world record was within my grasp. Duncan Shea-Simonds puts it like this:

Another fast marathon and some strong 70.3 races indicated that the record was doable, but like all long-course athletes Has had to walk the fine line between training enough and nursing niggles which would crop up along the way. Many of Haseeb's brilliant guides (Chris, Rupert, Kieron and others) helped during his preparations – but a big chunk of the work was completed on his own with many tedious hours spent training INDOORS.

Here, both the treadmill and the Wattbike had proven

invaluable. They allowed Has to train in relative safety, at the intensity required, for hours on end. I'm sure the resulting mind-numbing tedium must have played its part in giving Has the mental toughness he would undoubtedly need to draw upon.

Dunc and I walked through the archway and ran into the sea and then dived in head-first. Amazingly there were no nerves on my part. The calm Calella sea enabled me to get straight into a steady rhythmic stroke. I felt so relaxed, and I could sense that we were overtaking people as I occasionally brushed past them. Ten minutes in and someone accidently bashed me in the face with their hand and my goggles came slightly off my eye and let in water. It was a bit frustrating as I had to shut my right eye to stop the sea salt getting in and stinging. Despite not being able to see, it is still uncomfortable in the same way that it would be for anyone who can see.

During the swim Dunc and I were tethered calf-to-calf, with me on his right. We were passing people all the time, gaining places and making good time. I felt my hand on someone's shoulder at one point and couldn't help but use them as a lever to propel myself forward. *If only I could do this for the rest of the race*, I thought fleetingly, *but I guess that would be cheating.*

When we reached halfway Dunc and I stopped, as agreed as part of our race strategy, and he told me that we were now on the return leg. "We're doing really well, mate – forty-three minutes... that's fantastic."

I replied, "Cool, let's crack on."

A little further on and a woman obliviously swam between Dunc and me. We stopped and Dunc shouted out, "He's blind!"

"What?" she asked.

Dunc tried to explain, "He can't see." Pointing to my eyes.

"Oh," said the woman, but there was no time for any more polite conversation – after all we had come to race.

My left shoulder and neck began to ache. I only breathe on the right side of my body (turning my head slightly to the right find that pocket of air as my right arm begins to come out of the water at my hip) and swimming for over an hour was clearly putting a lot of stress on my left side. I really couldn't wait for the swim to be over at this stage. However, with the knowledge that we were over halfway and that the last bit back was going to be quicker I soldiered on. And sure enough, we eventually reached the shore and I was out in one hour, twenty-two minutes and thirty-nine seconds. Boom! This was around eighteen minutes quicker than my coach had predicted and took everyone by surprise. It actually led to family and friends almost missing us coming out of the water. We were off to a cracking start.

Our transition wasn't bad either. With wetsuits stripped off and bike gear on (helmet, cycle shorts and shoes), we were out of the changing tent in five minutes, and on our way to the mounting line. It was great to be racing on the Matrix tandem. I had bought it earlier in 2016 and I absolutely love it. With its Fast Forward wheels it started to shift pretty nicely and we settled into a steady twenty-three miles per hour pace once we wound our way out of Calella. I noticed it was very hot and made sure I drank plenty of fluids on the tandem. I had two bottles mounted behind me and one on the bar underneath me. We stopped once to pick up some more bottles of water. I made sure I poured some cool water into my helmet to stop me overheating. It felt refreshing and worked for about five minutes before I started to cook in the midday sun.

We overtook cyclist after cyclist. It felt great and so easy at first. Dunc's constant call to other competitors – "On your left!" – became a familiar chant throughout the bike leg as we were riding on the right-hand side of the road.

After fifty-six miles we arrived back through transition in two hours and thirty minutes, where we got some tremendous cheers. I felt adrenaline rush through my veins and blew a little kiss to some fans who were shouting out my name. I was to find out later that they were Irish. I have a very soft spot for Irish folk. My wife and her family are of Irish origin and I've been to Ireland on numerous occasions and just love the hospitality out there. And here it was again for Dunc and me.

On to the second lap. This was harder going, particularly the last hour or so. My back and neck felt like they were on fire with fatigue and my blackout goggles were digging into my face. Dunc and I got out of the saddle a number of times during the last hour of the bike leg to stretch our legs. The bike section seemed to be going on forever. It wasn't as if I could enjoy the scenery to take my mind off the constant discomfort. I just couldn't wait for it to end. It was such a relief to come back into transition and get off the bike. The bike leg took us five hours and eight minutes, so we were well ahead of schedule. I had dreams of knocking out an overall time of ten hours and thirty minutes, but the run was going to prove tougher than I had ever imagined. In all honesty I didn't really know how fatigued I was going to feel on the run or the levels of suffering I was to endure. I don't think anyone can prepare you mentally for the Ironman marathon. I was about to find out how much this was going to hurt.

Once in the transition tent Dunc handed me my bag, but it wasn't mine. It had a helmet in it instead of my shoes.

Confused, I asked, "Where's my shoes?"

In horror, Dunc said, "Oh no, mate, where's your shoes, Has?"

I replied, "I have no idea, buddy, you hung them up on the peg."

Dunc quickly realised that he had mistakenly picked up someone else's bag. I must admit that I had a mild panic and for a fleeting moment thought I might have to run the 26.2 miles in bare feet. Thankfully Dunc soon located my bag and I pulled on my socks and shoes. Dunc handed me one end of the run tether and off we went. It felt great initially, running out of the transition zone and on to the first of three laps of 26.2 miles.

I heard my lovely daughter Ayeisha call out to me, "You're doing really well!"

I shouted back, "Happy birthday, babe!" It was so lovely to hear her voice and it really lifted my spirits.

At this stage I was feeling okay as we started to knock off an eight minutes per mile pace. However, by mile six I hit the proverbial wall and had what I can only describe as some kind of meltdown. My legs felt heavy and my lungs felt like they were bursting. Dunc tried to keep the pace up and pulled on the tether. However, there was no way he would be able to pull me all the way around the twenty miles we had left, so he quickly relented and allowed me to slow down. I felt my shoes start to scuff the ground as I started the infamous Ironman shuffle.

"Pick up your feet, Has!" Dunc shouted to me. He describes those first few miles in his blog:

Once ready I guided Has over the various trip hazards and onto the run course. The opening mile was very congested and featured a number of twists, turns and surface changes – all opportunities for Has to lose his footing, trip or take a tumble.

Starting the marathon we were both feeling pretty confident. We'd set ourselves a 3:30–3:45 target. With Has having run a straight marathon in under 3 hours this was not at all unrealistic. We passed through the first mile in 8 minutes to the second. Bang on schedule but I could tell Haseeb had not found it comfortable. I hoped that his run legs would come to him, so kept the pace where it needed to be for a 3:30.

Mile 2, 8:06.
Mile 3, 8:09.
Mile 4, 8:01.

I was keeping the pace high, but I sensed Has was burning too many matches.

The pace dropped off considerably and I was seriously wondering whether I would finish. I felt godawful. If I was in the TV show *I'm a Celebrity… Get Me Out of Here!* I would have opted out for sure. It was the last place I wanted to be and I'd never felt as bad at this stage of a race in all of the competitions I had done. To give some context, I normally hit the wall in a marathon around twenty miles but now I had already hit it at six miles; what on earth was going on? I kept telling Dunc to slow down as I needed to recover; it was so hot and I was getting thirsty; I had consumed plenty of fluids on the tandem but still I was struggling and I was seriously wondering whether I would finish.

Dunc was doing his utmost to guide me through all the runners and obstacles and I know that at one point I had a near miss with a bollard when, uncharacteristically, Dunc lost his concentration. We finished lap one of three in one hour and twenty minutes and I was struggling big time. Dunc recalls:

Through the first lap in about 1 hr 15 minutes. I knew right then we wouldn't run the next 2 at that pace. Has was slowing with each mile and I was getting worried. Very worried.

I wasn't able to get my head around why I was feeling so rubbish. I obviously couldn't see the pain etched on the faces of many of the other Ironman competitors who were suffering as badly or worse than myself. Nor could I see those who were now walking. However, I could occasionally hear some of their laboured breathing and their heavy feet pounding the ground. Despite this it was difficult for me to forget my own extreme discomfort. I was hurting and this was going to go on for much longer than I wanted.

Dunc could see that I was getting very distressed at this stage. He was brilliant. He did his best to distract me away from the pain I felt by filling me in on what was happening around me. This was so very important in keeping me going. "Has, there are so many people walking, lots of casualties, mate." He also tried to get my mind off the pain and suffering. At one stage I heard *Sultans of Swing* by Dire Straits playing over the PA system. Dunc said he loved that song, and I said I preferred the *Making Movies* album.

With two more laps to go I knew I couldn't sustain a high-tempo pace. We were walking every aid station (the course has aid stations every two miles with drinks, gels and food for the athletes), which was a wonderful relief and it meant I could take a very brief rest and get some fluids on board. I stuck to Coke to ensure that I didn't develop any gastrointestial problems.

The second lap was even harder going than the first and I remember saying in utter desperation to Dunc, "I don't care about the world record any more."

His response was, "World records aren't meant to be easy, mate, that's why they are called world records; you will just have to suffer like a dog." All I wanted to do was walk for a few minutes and again Dunc stepped in and said that if I wanted to walk it was going to be a very long walk, and we hadn't come all this way just to walk. These words were an echo of what he had said to me five years previously in the London Marathon when I was about to throw in the towel. One thing was for sure – I wasn't going to get much sympathy from my guide. In Dunc's own words:

Coming to the end of lap two and Has slowed to a walk. A second or two passed. Right, it was time for me to go full bastard. I shouted, "Come on, Has – if we walk now it's gonna be a f***ing *long day." (Pardon my French but needs must.) I told him we just gotta keep running.*

Towards the latter part of the second lap my foot brushed the promenade wall and I fell onto my right quad and got a severe pain in my upper leg. As I lay there on the concrete momentarily, I thought to myself, *Game over*, and it was almost a relief – the chance to stop the suffering.

Dunc asked me if I was okay. "Is it cramp? If it is only cramp then get up and shake it out. It's best to run it off."

Run it off? I wanted desperately to stop and take some time out. This guy was unbelievable. I have to admit there were times I just wanted to punch him in the face, and this was one of those moments. But as I found out later post-race, even Dunc was very concerned that I might have done some serious damage.

I obediently did as I was told and got up and took a few tentative steps. Miraculously as I started to run the pain in my quad disappeared (no let-off for me then). On the third lap it was clear that I was going to keep running. There was a point where I did walk for about five seconds but then decided against it. I thought about the hard work Martin had put into collecting all the evidence and liaising with all the race officials. I thought about my daughter, who I so wanted to be proud of me, and family and friends at the race and at home who were supporting me. I thought about my coach Claire, who had been tweaking my training month in, month out to get the best performance out of me. Last but not least was of course Dunc, who was suffering just like me, who not only had to dig deep but was having to constantly encourage me to keep going. But when push came to shove, I knew I wasn't a quitter. When things have been tough I've always tried to battle through. I told myself that each mile done was one mile less than the last and a step closer to the finishing line.

But there was no getting away from the fact that the twists and turns on the course played their part in wearing me down. There were a number of 180-degree turns we had to negotiate. Dunc carefully guided me around, ensuring that I covered every inch of the course I needed to in order to accomplish our goal fair and square. Unfortunately not all the competitors wanted to stick to the course. To Dunc's complete disgust a number of them cut corners and didn't go around the turns as they should have. I heard Dunc shouting at them to stop cheating.

The last six miles were the most gruelling and seemed to go on forever, but somehow, from nowhere, I found an extra gear.

Even Dunc was surprised. "Come on, mate, keep this up and we could still do it. The world record is within our grasp."

I started to speed up, and to believe it was possible. As we knocked off each mile the prospect of setting a new world record seemed to get even closer.

"Come on, mate, we only have two miles to go. A lousy two miles… you've done that so many times round the block." Dunc was right, but I hadn't done it after 2.4 miles of swimming, 112 miles of biking and 24.2 miles of running. However, I just wanted to finish now so I put everything I had into my run. It was all so surreal. It was almost an out-of-body experience as the pain seemed to disappear and I felt like I was floating along. I shut my eyes and let Dunc provide the guiding commentary. I was on autopilot by now. From Dunc's perspective:

I knew I was already treading a fine line with Haseeb. But I also knew he had the propensity to soak up huge amounts of physical discomfort. Has was clearly close to the edge and pushing him any harder might mean 'nighty-night' – but we had to try.

The sun was now lower in sky and the air noticeably cooler. I

urged Has to focus on his gait – keeping it as efficient as possible.
The last 5 miles I don't think I shut up. I kept telling Has we could
still do it.

We could do it... I knew we could... I believed it... I just had
to make Has believe it!

Yet, with only one mile to go the situation changed again. The
last mile stretched on forever, or so it seemed. The pain racked
my battered body and tore at my mind. Perhaps it was because I
could hear the crowds cheering and I just wanted that finishing
line to be underneath my aching feet. I knew in my head that the
suffering would soon stop.

Eight hundred metres to go... then two hundred... and
then, "Has, we are going to turn into the finishing shoot!"

That last hundred metres couldn't come quickly enough.
Dunc was absolutely elated, putting his arm around me as we
ran to the finish line; he was shoving me in the back (only for a
couple of seconds) and shouting, "You've done it, woo-hoo!" I
was so happy, but completely spent.

Paul Kaye, the voice of Ironman, boomed over the PA
system, "Haseeb Ahmad, you are an Ironman. You have broken
the blind Ironman record by almost seven minutes!"

As soon as I crossed the finishing line my legs gave up and I
was whisked away to the medical tent where I just lay, unable to
communicate, and when I got up I just wanted to throw up! I felt
pig-sick.

"Come on, mate, let's get out of the tent, buddy. You'll get a
lot more sympathy out there than you will from me in here."

I so wanted to walk out of the tent but every time I got up I
felt really ill. I didn't want to be sick in front of everyone! While
I was lying there, quite helpless, Dunc was questioning his role
in my current state:

I followed Has into the med tent where, overcome with nausea, he was tended to for 30 minutes or so. I went off to gather our dry clothes and returned to the tent where Has was now spark out on the recovery couch. Looking at him lying there totally wasted did make me question what we'd done.

What I'd MADE him do...

Guiding a blind athlete, who you class as a dear friend, around an Ironman in an attempt to break a world record is pretty strange gig and it's one I'm not sure I've got my head around yet.

Although the best of friends, when I'm guiding Has, I'm doing a job. I'm not his friend. In fact I'm probably his worst nightmare... Ironman just magnifies the whole process tenfold.

I suppose a 'friend' might have seen Haseeb suffering and if it was in their power to make it stop... they would have.

When Has wanted to walk, a friend might have let him.

When he wanted to take longer in the aid stations and drink a litre of Coke, a friend would have opened the bottle.

What kind of friend yanks someone to their feet and makes them start running, when their legs are cramping having just fallen arse over tit onto a concrete wall?

Who needs a friend like that?

People who wanna break Ironman world records I suppose!

It was the hardest sporting challenge of my life. I knew it was going to be extremely difficult but until you personally experience an Ironman race you never really appreciate the amount of mental strength you need just to pull through. I never dreamt that I would set a world record. I used to watch the TV show *Record Breakers* as a kid and was amazed at the way in which people of all ages and backgrounds would set themselves seemingly impossible challenges. Now it was my turn to make the impossible possible.

Once I was out of the medical tent (which seems to be one of my favourite post-race hang-out places) I made my way through the reception tent. Dunc and I got a standing ovation from all the other athletes. It was so moving.

One of the Spanish officials came across and apologised for her lack of fluent English and said, "I'm so proud that you have broken the world record here in Barcelona. Well done."

I felt so ill that I wasn't able to enjoy the moment at all really. But no one can say I didn't put it all out there on the course. Months and months of training, blood, sweat and toil and now I hold the world record for the fastest Ironman for a totally blind athlete. How about that?

We decided to make our way to the Shea-Simonds' apartment as a halfway point for me to rest and recover but before we were able to reach the flat, Ayeisha had to run into a shop to get a bag for me to throw up into. Once the contents of my stomach (which wasn't a lot) were emptied I felt a whole lot better.

We flew back the following day into Luton. I really wished I had stayed on another couple of days for the closing ceremony, especially as Paul Kaye, who made the presentations, gave Dunc and me a special mention. Such a lovely touch, such a phenomenal race and such lovely people. I can't thank everyone enough for all their support on the course and off it. I would definitely go back and do this race again one day. Despite the fact that all the way through the run I said I would never do another Ironman!

ACKNOWLEDGEMENTS

There have been a number of people who have been instrumental in helping me during the final stages in the production of my book. Their contributions have been invaluable to give me critical feedback, resulting in the odd tweak here and there. There are too many to name individually so here I would like to thank them all for their time and energy reading my original manuscript. I really appreciated all of your feedback to me.

I do, however, want to thank a few specific people who contributed significantly to the development of the book. Tim Heming for his eloquently and brilliantly written foreword; what an amazing and talented writer you are, Tim. It was a privilege getting to know you while pounding the streets of Leicester and London together. Thanks also go to my guides Rupert, Andrew, Rodger, Chris, and Dunc who all kindly offered their contributions to the book. A big thanks and hugs to my brother Shazib for his touching account of his memories of his older brothers in chapter 5.

A massive thanks for the great photos from Barcelona taken by my lovely friends Martin and Joanna Westall and to Janet Shea-Simonds for the amazing photo of Rupert and I tiptoeing through the mud - I wish it had been tulips!

I cannot end the acknowledgements without special mention of those who have supported me in my life and helped me become the person I am today. So, thank you Mum, Dad, my brothers and sister. In my triathlon career I want to thank Jonny Riall at British Triathlon, the numerous guides who have contributed to my success as an athlete and the Guide Dog Association for their support in training both me and my beautiful and clever Guide Dogs, Quin and Walt. A special mention goes also to all those who have looked after my guide dogs over the years including Heather Lydall and Abby Reynolds. And, last but not least, I want to thank all of my colleagues who have helped me in my career, some of whom have become personal friends outside the world of work.

I also would like to thank Matador Publishers for their help and assistance in the production of the book. A special acknowledgement to Chris Mawer, of HE Translations, for the final proofread and some little but important copyediting changes at the final stage of the proofreading process. This was undoubtedly aided by the fact that Chris was a very special Ironman triathlete in her day too.

And finally, a thank-you to you, my readers; I hope my book did not prove to be such a tough challenge of endurance for you as that long day in Barcelona was for me!